Trawlers and Trawler Folk

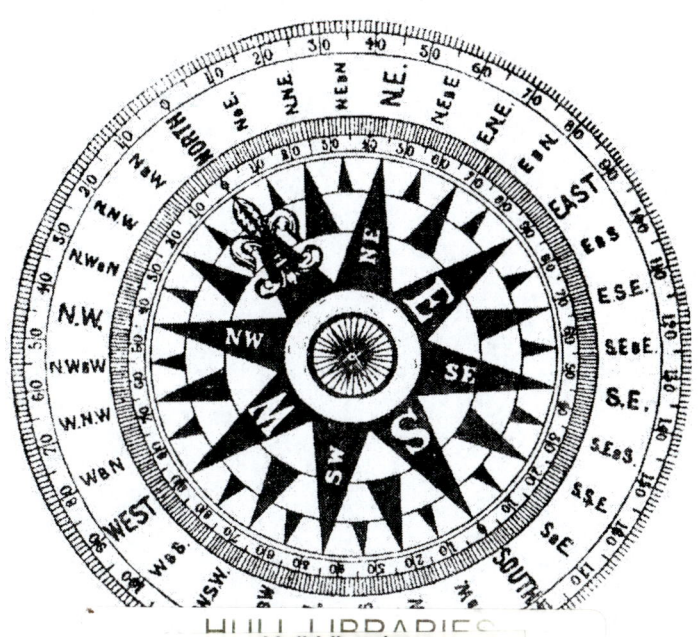

Trawlers and Trawler Folk

Ernest Cleveland

PNEUMA SPRINGS PUBLISHING UK

First Published in 2009 by:
Pneuma Springs Publishing

Trawlers and Trawler Folk
Copyright © 2009   Ernest Cleveland
ISBN: 978-1-905809-67-7

Contribution and Editing by:
Barrie Cleveland, Jonathan Monk & Margaret Monk

Pneuma Springs Publishing
A Subsidiary of Pneuma Springs Ltd.
7 Groveherst Road, Dartford Kent, DA1 5JD.
E: admin@pneumasprings.co.uk
W: www.pneumasprings.co.uk

A catalogue record for this book is available from the British Library.

Published in the United Kingdom. All rights reserved under International Copyright Law. Contents and/or cover may not be reproduced in whole or in part without the express written consent of the publisher.

This book was written by Ernest Cleveland
with additional material from his son Barrie Cleveland and
editing by daughter Margaret and grandson Jonathan Monk.

Ernest also thanks his brother Charles, an ex trawler skipper, who initially helped in the creation of this book, being a factual record covering a period of twenty-five years experience in the Hull Fishing Industry.

Most of the photographs and drawings are from Ernest's collection; therefore the origin of some is unknown.

1939

The author in the uniform of a junior officer of the Merchant Navy – Fishing Section. The band on the cuff was green in colour. A uniform was essential if the vessel was armed, otherwise the crew were considered to be pirates.

ABOUT THE AUTHOR

Ernest was born into a fishing tradition in Kingston upon Hull in 1910 at 3 Park View cottages, Diversion Rd.

His father, as his grandfather and great grandfather before him, was a fisherman originating from Margate in Kent in the mid 19th century.

Whilst his father was at sea Ernest's mother died when he was just eight years of age thus leaving him, his three brothers and his sister alone. He then had to find help and St Vincent's, one of many orphanages in the city, answered the call. Ernest, along with his three brothers, was looked after by the Sisters of Charity.

At the age of fourteen he left St Vincent's and, as many others did, signed up as deckie learner on his first deep sea trawler heading for Iceland, spending the next 15 years in the fishing industry and achieving a boatswain's ticket in 1930.

At the outbreak of war in 1939, Ernest then moved into the Merchant Navy Fishing section and eventually into the Royal Navy (Harry Tate's Navy), mostly doing escort duty in the Indian Ocean.

While stationed in Ipswich, Ernest met Dorothy Pulham and in 1942 they married. At the end of the war they set up home in Hull, and Ernest went back to fishing until 1950 when he continued his link with the sea by taking a position as Fishery Officer with the North Eastern Sea Fisheries Committee. This involved a move to Hartlepool with his wife, son and daughter. In Hartlepool the couple completed their family with another son.

Ernest retired in 1975 and began to devote his spare time to his family and to his hobbies of painting and writing his memoirs.

When Ernest died in 1985 his book had not been published. In 2007 we decided to undertake the task of editing his memoirs for publication and incorporating supporting information from our own researches.

Barrie Cleveland, Margaret and Jonathan Monk
(son, daughter and grandson)

CONTENTS

1 My Grandfather and life in the fishing community as a child
2 My early sea trips; fleet fishing; technological advances and new, distant fishing grounds
3 Arctic fishing conditions; accidents and emergencies at sea
4 Sea rescue; changes in fishing patterns; spectacular storms
5 Faroe Islands and whaling; emergency repairs at sea; developing technologies; relations between skippers and owners
6 Fishing off Iceland; the fate of HMS Rawalpindi; washed overboard
7 Illegal fishing; polar ice; life on board; life onshore between trips
8 The hazards of bad weather
9 Fishing diversification; unusual catches
10 Fishing off Greenland; icebergs; landing the catch
11 The fishing community in Hull; returning to Iceland; reminiscences of Iceland fishing; ship hulls
12 Fishing in the White Sea; training at Hull Nautical School
13 Fishing off Lapland; depth sounding technology
14 Developing technologies; catching Gannets; my new passion for motorcycling; back to Iceland
15 Competition between trawlers; vessels lost at sea, seizing life onshore, exploratory voyages
16 Iceland in the 1920's; Christmas in the fishing community; sailing on the Cape Matapan in bad conditions
17 Difficult winter trips; sailing as mate; changes in the fishing industry after my time

Appendix 1

Map of Barents Sea showing Bear Island

This statue, known as the "Fishermen's Memorial", stands at the corner of the Boulevard on Hessel Road, Hull and commemorates one of the most celebrated events in the history of the Fishing Fleets of Hull.

On the 22nd October 1904 the Imperial Russian Navy was in the North Sea in the area of the Dogger Bank fishing grounds when it came across several vessels of the Gamecock fleet from Hull. It was claimed that these fishing boats were mistaken for the Japanese Navy ships being hunted and the Russian Fleet opened fire for twenty minutes. The statue is thought to represent George Smith, skipper of the *Crane* which was sunk as he tried to halt the shelling from the deck of his ship.

CHAPTER ONE

It was through listening spellbound to my grandfather's stirring and often told tales of his lifetime at sea in the fishing smacks of the period 1880 to 1915, sailing the North Sea and distant waters, that decided my future, however strongly my father (also a trawler skipper) tried to discourage me. Being unable to read or write, my grandfather, like many of his kind, skippered smacks to sea, netted a quantity of fish and returned home by the sole means of sails and manpower. It was their way of life and their livelihood. To lay off a course on their ancient vaguely drawn charts, matchsticks were laid in line from point to point, which gave a measure of the distance too. In those days, a beginner had to join a smack as cook then work his way up. The skipper's ticket was a servitude one showing time served sea-going. Incidentally, it was my grandfather who devised and first used a towing block, a device which held the trawl warps above the propeller to enable the vessel to manoeuvre, greatly reducing the risk of having a trawl warp cut or tangled round the prop (a nasty predicament, especially in bad weather).

My grandfather was almost as broad as he was high, and a stern disciplinarian: a flippant answer to a query would bring a strong rebuke. There was a selection of meerschaum pipes in a wall rack next to a large barometer encased in brass, awarded for bravery at sea in rescuing the crew of a smack. There was a heavy leather belt draped over a chair he always slept in. I once handled the belt, he told me that was the proper place for it, never to wear one, and that he had never had a good reason to use it. The mere sight of such a chastiser was sufficient to make me behave myself.

The women folk of this community lived a lifetime of hardship and hard work. Their time away from housework was fully occupied in knitting thick, white abbs (fishermen's underwear), sea boot stockings and blue or white Guernseys (*Ganseys*). In fine weather this would be done in the company of neighbours sitting on high backed chairs outside their front doors.

Ernest's Great Grandfather James, Great Uncles John and Charles and Grandfather Richard

The whole street of terraced houses huddled together housing one big family, with practically all the men folk sea-going or to do with ships. In every front window were the aspidistra and the model ship and in the background was the gleam of polished brass. Heavy ornate velvet draped the mantelpiece under which was a long brass rod for drying and airing clothes. Every house had its rocking chair but even well into the 1920's many had neither gas, electricity nor flush toilets. All the year round, large coal fires were a necessity. The fireplaces shone with black lead and brass fire irons. Outside, doorsteps were stoned daily and the pavement scrubbed down to the curb-stones. Few women possessed a coat; a knitted shawl was fashionable, popular and easily made.

I remember one amusing incident my grandfather used to relate with a chuckle; late one night he was surprised to hear heavy rainfall striking the large tin bath that hung outside the kitchen window. Puzzled, since his weather glass had never let him down before; he tapped it before going outside to find one of his sons using his bedroom window instead of coming down to the yard.

One yarn was of a lad who started sea-going as cook and on his first night he forgot to soak the peas for the following day. This forgetfulness upset the crew, naturally, so he had to place a pan of peas on the deck one side of the rigging and an empty pan on the opposite side, he then had to transfer the peas from one pan to the other by taking one pea at a time, up the rigging and down the other side. Another drastic punishment could have ended in tragedy when one member of the crew was, for a short while, towed astern alongside the trawl. Some voyages to distant grounds could last over several weeks making the maintenance of discipline difficult.

CHAPTER TWO

On leaving school in 1924, at the age of thirteen, my life at sea began as a 'deckie' learner on an Icelandic-bound trawler from the port of Hull. The duration of each trip was three weeks more or less from dock to dock, the catches being packed on ice. The return journey to Iceland generally took about eight days and nights, when steaming around ten knots, and thirteen days on the fishing grounds, not always fishing. Conditions and the weather had to be reckoned with. Weekly wages were paid, plus a small share of the sum the catch sold for, less the vessel's expenses. If the total realised was insufficient to meet the expenses, the crew had the privilege of contributing a share to meet them, for having been on board. At that time (1926) most vessels had paraffin oil or carbide lamps as the only means of lighting, while some were slowly being equipped with dynamos. To hoist a paraffin light to the masthead in a rough sea would try the patience of Job. I've seen the most placid go berserk, and the most resolute reduced to the depths of despair trying to achieve this. After two trips, my next venture was to sign on a smaller steam trawler of one of the two remaining boxer fleets. Each fleet was made up of about twenty-five smallish steam trawlers: one was the Red Cross fleet, having a red cross on their funnels, the other the Gamecock with the namesake on their funnels.

The vessels were at sea for five to six weeks and fished in convoys. Each fleet had an Admiral in the leading ship and the rest trawled astern. They did not have enough power to turn or manoeuvre if dragging a trawl on one side, so, by the use of a bridle, the trawl was towed dead astern. Steering either way then was no problem; however when stern trawling became popular in the 1970's it was proclaimed as a new method. Crews consisted of five above deck, a cook and three engine men: all turned-to for boarding operations. Two vessels used for ferrying fish, known as cutters, worked with the fleets, regularly taking the boxes of fish (pads) to the London market, Billingsgate. Every morning, weather permitting, the Admiral's boarding flag was hoisted, all fishing stopped and the vessels' boats (coggies) were launched to ferry the catches, boxed and ready for sale, across to the cutters. This could be hazardous, dangerous work, depending on the weather. The sea was alive with boats, their men rowing and shouting, carrying, at times, up to forty or fifty boxes in each boat to transfer to the cutters, which took more than one trip. The boxes of fish showing the vessels names had to be manhandled into the boats and again dragged inboard over the bulwarks on board the cutters. The sea had to be very rough for the fleet to miss a day's boarding. There was also a missionary ship to serve both fleets. This ship had provision for rendering first aid on board and dealt with the welfare, reading and other crew's comforts under the flag of the Royal National Mission to Deep Sea Fishermen. Wherever this flag is flown, it commands the respect and admiration of all true fishermen.

A few skippers would deliberately lose the fleet, slip away to seek better fishing and then rejoin it for boarding. They sometimes succeeded. The Admiral knew, but followed Nelson's example. Being an Admiral was a tremendous responsibility, as can be realised. Vessels were always leaving or returning to the fleet, which was continually at sea, often well off the Danish coast, thus allowing letters to be sent or received, also the odd newspaper, in order to keep in touch with fish prices. This type of fishing eventually became uneconomic and both fleets were laid up in 1936 to be eventually sold and dispersed to various ports.

By 1920 it was becoming difficult to find good profitable catches from the North Sea, and more trawlers were going to distant grounds: Iceland, The Faroe Isles, Norwegian Coast and the area off the White Sea. The sizes of the vessels were being increased to carry larger catches and more fuel. To carry sufficient fuel for distant waters, the vessel's aft fish room had to be filled with coal. The coal was then taken from there, through a tunnel, to the stokehold. When emptied, the fish room was thoroughly washed out (hard work all round) so it could again be used for its initial purpose. Oil burners, when coal was superseded, were a major advancement.

After a few years, in 1930, when these grounds had become well fished, the prolific waters around Bear Isle, North of Norway, thirteen hundred miles from the Humber, were opened up. By this time the trawlers were much larger and better equipped. Some had depth sounding instruments, all had dynamos and a few could carry sufficient water to have a couple of hip baths on board, and if not built as oil burners, were quickly being converted from coal. Another useful aid which nearly all trawlers now had was steam steering gear which simplified steering by doing away with fighting a bucking hand steering wheel and lashing with strops in bad weather. This meant better handling of the ship in tight areas. Most vessels were also using a more efficient method of trawling by using French gear with Dan Lines and ground cables added to the other trawl, almost doubling its effective catching area.

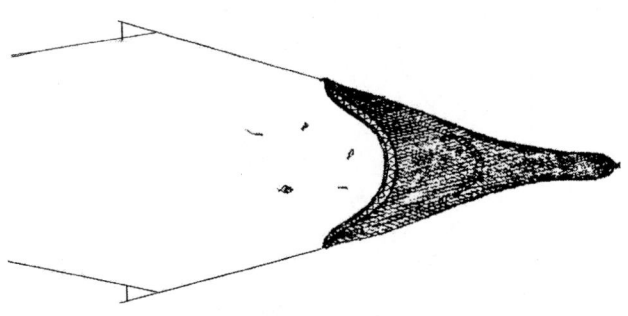

Basic trawl using French gear

On my first voyage to Bear Isle, the fish, mainly cod, were very dense and good catches were made over many years, whilst further afield, Spitzbergen and Nova Zemla proved to have good fishing grounds. At first the fish were found to be full of a certain kind of seaweed they fed on, which contained a deal of iodine, and not all early catches sold. However, as proved to be the case on other new grounds, the quality greatly improved when the immense shoals of cod were thinned out by the onslaught of fishing.

When fishing in prolific waters, the trawl was shot and hauled after a sweep round. It was a case of 'dip and fill' hauling in full trawls and getting on deck around twelve bags of fish, each holding about three hundred stone. Sometimes we had to lay with a net alongside full of fish until the decks had been cleared sufficiently to give them space. It did not take much of a rough sea to create havoc. Tons of fish were lost when nets tore away under the weight of the catch, apart from those lost overboard when full up to the gunwales or teemed overboard as the vessel rolled. It is impossible to give any idea of the enormous quantities wasted: shoals were decimated. It was wholesale slaughter, a huge ruthless massacre. A deck load of fish was sometimes dumped if the sun had been on it a while, but this did not matter as it was quickly refilled. Oh! We fishermen, how foolish we were, how short sighted; the damage we inflicted on those shoals of cod finally caught up with us. Too late, we learnt the bitter truth: just what we had done on our quest for gold could never be undone.

The seas were not inexhaustible, no matter how often the elements threw all their furious energies of ice and storms in defence. Ships and crews were obliterated, as if they had never existed, and the scars and wounds of these battles with nature will last for many more years to come. A terrible price was paid, over many years, in various ways. Inevitably the 'gold rush' eventually petered out; Greenland and the great Newfoundland banks, however, were still to come, ripe for plundering.

CHAPTER THREE

The weather over the winter months in the Arctic was often treacherous and violent. The winters lasted so long, nearly six months, much of which time there was complete darkness, yet in midsummer it was just the reverse: then shone the midnight sun. The sky could rapidly change from terrifying to magnificent, the sea from greenish black to marvellous shades of blue. Most feared and dreaded was the onset of black frost in the guise of freezing fog, which would envelop the vessel in darkness, forming a thick ice coating over and around everything.

About to haul the trawl, Barents Sea

Axes were the only effective weapon against this deadly menace. Should one side of the vessel ice up more than the other an awful list developed, which, if unable to be checked, meant a gradual keeling over, and finally turning turtle and plunging to the sea bed. Many ships were lost in this way, as no help or assistance was possible.

When the icy fog engulfed a vessel it was all hands on deck wielding axes to control this monster. Hot water only made matters worse, freezing as it left the hoses. It was amazing how one could displace the huge chunks of ice with the right approach and manhandle them over the rail. We improved with practice and were soon experts with the axe: not surprising when our lives were at stake! It was very warm work. Nevertheless, in one such battle against overwhelming odds we noticed a young learner, motionless: this could have been fatal. When we grabbed him he was as stiff as a corpse, but he soon thawed out when we put him next to the galley stove. Our methods in difficult situations were often crude and drastic, but speedy and effective. The onset of ice could differ enormously, sometimes appearing like thousands of snow-white swans with heads held high, floating majestically in deep blue ponds, or sailing ships dipping and tossing as the wind filled their sails driving them along in a choppy blue sea. It could also be awesome and frightening when the icebergs came along like towering buildings, grey and streaked with black. In a rough sea they would rise and fall, pushing forth bow waves like a large ship. They could be extremely noisy. When the submerged part melted the top weight caused them to roll over with a tremendous noise and splash.

As might be expected, accident and ill health problems of crewmembers were fairly common. Difficulties often arose in attempting to help the unfortunate. One vessel went aground in heavy snow showers whilst negotiating a passage through the Lofoten Islands to take an injured man to the nearest hospital. A member of one of my crews had a leg torn off when the trawl came fast to an obstruction on the seabed, stopping the vessel in its wake. Snagging of nets like this often caused something to give and on this occasion a bollard broke and the warp (trawl wire) zipped across the man's leg. After standing him in a bag of flour, to stop the bleeding, we got the gear aboard and made for the nearest port, which was over thirty miles distant, in order to gain urgent medical help. Despite rough weather we, miraculously, made it and the man lived – in a similar accident in other circumstances, two men had been killed. These happenings show a two hundred mile fishing limit is unjust, on humanitarian grounds. Consider a victim of a serious accident, or a vessel urgently needing shelter, perhaps crippled from a storm, or wanting mechanical repairs, that is a long distance to cover in any circumstances.

Many such cases can be recalled. One in particular was a certain deck-hand who was taken seriously ill aboard a vessel fishing in the vicinity of Bear Isle. Hospital aid was many miles away and the weather was foul. Fortunately, this was after wireless had been installed in many boats so the worried skipper, concerned, contacted other skippers by radio for advice. A skipper of a Russian trawler broke into the conversation to say he had a doctor on board and if several ships laid to windward, thereby shielding his vessel from the pounding seas, he would launch a boat and send his doctor across to see the man. This was done and the sick man was found to be in urgent need of an appendectomy, which was duly performed successfully on board the Russian vessel. When recovered he was returned to his own ship, owing his life to that doctor and many others.

A vessel could lose a few days valuable fishing time in the taking of a member of the crew into a port for medical reasons, or for any other matter. It was not lightly undertaken without good reason or consideration by any skipper. It could make all the difference between a financially good trip and a bad one. Occasionally, a man had to be left in a foreign hospital, even when his ship sailed for home.

CHAPTER FOUR

A Grimsby trawler, steaming out to Bear Isle, off course due to not having sighted anywhere on passage, made a landfall in extremely bad weather conditions, under the high land on the west side of the island, grounding firmly on the sea battered rocks. When the S.O.S was transmitted and picked up, a few skippers attempted the highly dangerous task, in appalling conditions, to reach the vessel by running out sea anchors and backing their ships, edging inshore towards the stricken ship and its crew. Though courageous and commendable, this action was doomed to failure: one ship almost landed beside the stranded one.

Several skippers decided that the only plan likely to succeed, though fraught with numerous perils, was to muster off the lee shore, launch their boats and send crew volunteers ashore to cross the isle, on foot, with ropes and tackle. At great risk, this was done and quite an invasion took place.

The only occupants of the island were two wireless operators manning a radio station there. It was dark with a near gale blowing when the men successfully landed only to find deep snow everywhere, to add to their almost insurmountable difficulties. Travelling in sea boots, carrying lights, ropes and other gear in the freezing cold of an Arctic night they fought their way, floundering through drifts and gullies until they finally got to a point above the doomed vessel and hauled the exhausted crew to safety. There were many acts of heroism that night but it was all part of a nights work. That it was completed successfully without the loss of a ship's boat or man was incredible.

One skipper was so determined to succeed, that when given a ship after a long spell ashore, and finding good fishing at Bear Isle, filled all the fish rooms, then ordered that the net and rope hold be cleared into the forecastle and filled the net store with fish up to the hatches. On the voyage home, the men could not have any heating in case it melted the ice and affected the fish stowed close to their quarters. Needless to say, the ship was grossly overloaded and was lucky to reach port again, where an inquiry was instituted.

The larger trawler crews varied slightly in number, there were four engine room ratings, a cook and twelve above deck, sometimes with a sparks (radio-operative) and a deckie learner. Prior to 1930 cod catches were not worth seeking, only prime fish, flat fish, haddock and hake, but now the filleting trade was opening up, cod was becoming more popular. When Fleetwood trawlers would only fish for hake, it was because at that port hake was the accepted fish, having a good demand, but times changed as the yield of the hake grounds declined, and the public's preferences had to change, if they wanted fish at all.

On one trip, a little more than halfway on our homeward run from Iceland to the Pentland Firth with a moderate catch of fish on board bound for the Humber, we encountered freakish bad weather. Vivid forked lightning streaked across the sky and torrential rain cascaded down the bridge windows. Suddenly the ship heeled over. What appeared to be a huge ball of fire had plunged into the sea a short distance off the starboard bow. The wheelhouse compass needle began spinning like a top, a check on the outside pole compass showed the same violent motion. One in the chartroom had also gone haywire and when the ship's lifeboat compass was brought out, and the four compared when they had finally settled down, all gave completely different readings, none of which could be relied upon.

Trusting to the known direction of the wind, hoping that there would be no appreciable change during the next 20 hours or so, our run continued through hazy, inclement weather and we were greatly relieved when the Orkney Isles were sighted. We put into harbour where the compass adjusters found they had no easy task. Reluctantly, some hours later we were allowed to leave with firm instructions to make port again if any compass deviation was noticed. The hull of the vessel had taken an exceptionally severe electrical charge, which had affected the magnetism. We reached our homeport without further incident, and for several months afterwards adjusters paid regular visits to the vessel until the hull was back to normal.

I have no doubt that had the thunderbolt fallen on board our fate would have been, as those of several vessels over the years have become, 'a mystery of the sea'.

Ernest served on the Cape Barfleur between 1932 and 1938, latterly for the Hudson Brothers

CHAPTER FIVE

The Orkney and Shetland Islands provided good fishing grounds, along with the group of many rocky islands, actually forty-two in number, which are situated conveniently halfway between Scotland and Iceland.

The Faroe Isles, like Iceland, have withstood over a century of activities by visiting fishing vessels. The Faroes were notorious for strong running tides, which made trawling haphazard in certain areas. Once, towing along in fine weather off Mygganes, we were suddenly caught up in a swirling tidal race and swept along in its grip. Decks awash, out of control, the vessel was swept right round the headland, passing almost underneath the Lighthouse, before the tide released its deadly hold. It was a very harrowing experience. Some old trawlers of low engine horsepower used to wait at anchor in the islands until the tides were slack. Whatever the direction of the wind, there was always a lee to be found and it was generally easy to change from one side of the isles to the other by steaming between them. A very large type of cod, were often found on Nolso Bank. They had unusually big heads, and each fish weighed up to four stone, so we were unable to throw them about the deck. Almost all kinds of good quality fish were to be found around these isles, but strangely one certain bank was well known as Lousy Bank as most of the fish trawled up here, even large halibuts, were infected and being slowly eaten away alive by swarms of some kind of small moving red lice, which fascinated us.

Trangisvaag, a village in the Faroe Isles which had once been a whaling station, consisted of well spread out houses built mainly of wood and upon stilts of a sort, so they provided shelter for poultry, sheep, goats and pigs, which were kept underneath, on the ground floor as it were. Narrow sparkling waterfalls tumbled down the mountain sides passing between the houses, to link up with the fjord many feet below. The Danes brought great benefits here, and also in Iceland and Greenland, particularly in the field of hospitals and schools.

Whilst undergoing an enforced stay in Trangisvaag's small hospital run by Danish doctors and nurses living in the village, I learned of an interesting local event which took place annually for many years. At about the same time each year, a number of whales entered the fjord, possibly to breed. However, when several were well inside, the entrance was blocked off by quickly placing a dam of timber across thereby trapping them. Then the whole village went to work, driving them aground, killing and capturing all they could. The villagers then celebrated for a whole week. As the village had been a whaling station, the whales were soon put to good use.

It was when abreast of the distant Faroes bound for Iceland that the trawler *The Cape Kanin's* engines had a major breakdown, probably due to the propeller thrashing the air whenever the stern lifted out of the water as she reared and plunged into deep troughs in the heaving sea. Unable to call for assistance, not yet having wireless, emergency repairs were soon in hand. A sea anchor was run out and a few deckhands went below to help while the remainder anxiously peered down from above; it was galling just to wait and hope, and an unenviable position for all to be in. A cylinder head had badly blown, and the holding-down bolts had gone: some had sheared off leaving the stumps behind, and though spare bolts were carried, it was practically impossible to fit them with the tools available. After several nerve-wracking hours, the engine room staff had done their best and the crew were told to bring along the fish room's wooden pound boards, which were used to separate the fish into box-like compartments. These were piled on top of the cylinder head as an added support to the bolts, right up high to the engine room top. When this was completed the engines were turned over and all seemed to be holding until she took a deep dive. There was a bang followed by an awful clattering as timber showered down, all over the engine room amid dense clouds of scalding steam. Fortunately, we had had the foresight to stand clear so no-one was hurt. The ensuing language was pretty strong but when peace and calm were restored in that confined space, despite the efforts of the vessel to thwart us, the whole operation was carefully and determinedly repeated. The restacked timber was firmly fixed with every wedge on board; each one hammered home so that if anything gave again it must be the engine room casing. This time, perhaps in answer to someone's prayers, the job held, enabling the vessel to limp into the isles for urgent repairs.[1]

In one noisy old trawler, the wrinkled-faced chief engineer, when told that we feared his 'sewing machines' would collapse, drew on his pipe, chuckled loudly and said, "Even in my bunk, I do know nothing is running hot". Never the less everyone else unlucky enough to be on board knew how noisy his engines were. Yet strangely, they held together as in one clattering contraption, defiant and contradictory, brazenly hissing puffs of steam in derision.

Trawler-men could, and often did, carry out minor repairs, which did not need a well-rigged workshop. It was surprising what they did manage to accomplish with the limited equipment on board, as not many were trained engineers in those days. To we seamen, the engines were known as "Three legged, up and down jobs", and they proved over many years to be extremely efficient and very reliable and would "run for ever". They altered little over a very long period; the first major change came around 1931 when super-heating was introduced. The steam was super heated before passing into the cylinders and it was feared at the time that this dry steam would scour the cylinder walls, thus shortening their lifetime; whether it had that effect is open to question. From

---
[1] To digress, a similar breakdown happened to me some years later, in 1942, when on a troop cum cargo ship, S.S. Themistocles. This engine was a "four-legged job". In this case one complete leg was dismantled and that part blocked off. The weather was perfect but the convoy had left us behind, a sitting duck for a wandering U-Boat. However, after some hours of anxiety, the engine repairs were finished and we were able to continue our voyage "on three legs" until Cape Town was reached. It is only fair to ention, the engine men were skilled engineers with the tools and the means.

coal to oil burning was the next modernisation until recent years, when in 1970 diesel engines began replacing the steam engines. Outwardly the design and layout was modernised fairly often, the aft end placed wheelhouse was moved amidships, whalebacks were fitted over the fore end, wheelhouses were extended, boat decks and wireless rooms incorporated, oil-fired boilers were used and eventually, the major change was made towards stern trawling.

By the end of 1931, quite a number of the larger trawlers had been equipped with wireless, receiving and transmitting in Morse. As a result another crew member had to be engaged: a wireless operator. At first, these men were big ship Marconi men who did not take too kindly to these smaller vessels, but they were most welcome on board. Direction finders were also fitted and found to be very useful in plotting position by the radio bearings beamed out from shore stations. Also the Walkers Patent Log that registered the mileage and streamed from the stern was being replaced by electrically operated logs, which registered on the bridge, a most useful innovation which saved the necessity of having a man to read the log on every watch, the procedure of which was a very dangerous one in bad weather as the log was positioned on the stern rail. Men were lost overboard just trying to do this duty. Some time later, radiotelephones replaced the early wireless sets and a 'sparks' was no longer compulsory. The skippers were permitted to operate those after qualifying at the end of a short training period. Listening to some of their chit chat could often be highly amusing: if the call "Hello, Hello, Ladies Lav" was heard, it was the trawler *"Lady Lavinia"* being contacted. Some calls were not so printable and the G.P.O had to moderate the language, mainly because the members of the public could, and often did, eavesdrop by purchasing special long wave sets for the purpose.

Radio, though a boon in many ways, could also prove otherwise to many skippers, as much longer range sets meant that vessels could be contacted direct from the company's office on the dock. This meant that, instead of complete freedom to fish wherever the skipper wished, because of regular reports passing to and fro from office to ship and vice versa, activities were severely curtailed. Firms had their charts divided into squares, each lettered and numbered in code, and then they were able to direct skippers from one place to another according to the daily reports from their vessels on the fishing grounds. In many instances, this method often failed to achieve the desired result and upset the morale of many men and drove some skippers to distraction. A report of a good catch would be flashed home resulting in messages going out to ships, perhaps many miles from the given position, causing considerable disruption and discord amongst vessels otherwise engaged. Fishing is (to put it mildly) very unpredictable and contrary. On receiving an order to proceed to square H.1., a trawler often arrived there to find 'the fish had flown'. It was incredible that huge dense shoals of fish could be around, there for the taking, suddenly to vanish completely from the area, yet unfailingly, over the years, they make cumulative seasonal appearances in certain places (e.g. the well known UK mackerel season) but these seasons can vary from year to year.

Most skippers either followed hunches or previous years' results according to the time of the year and the weather expected and in some cases, by direct reports from vessels working the distant grounds. A vessel sighted on its way home was signalled and information exchanged. There were so many points to consider before committing oneself to a definite course of action. The right decision meant a successful trip, which everyone wanted, and the men on the spot could judge the position and decide the outcome. An obvious solution to the problem of interference from the office, which worked for a time when first tried, was to cause the sets to be out of order, but the reshipping of a sparks discouraged this crafty practice. On another occasion, which illustrates the owner's attitude, a skipper was proudly surveying his large catch of cod, spread over a good proportion of the fish market, displayed for sale. He was sporting a gold watch and chain across the breadth of his waistcoat, very fashionable in those days, plain evidence of success, when the vessel's notoriously tyrannical owner appeared on the scene. He approached the skipper and remarked, "Nice watch and chain you have there, new is it?" The skipper, nonplussed, replied, "Yes, as a matter of fact it is". "I expect you look after it?" said the owner, "Yes", was the obvious reply. "Well just remember this, I provided that, along with your catches. I hope that you look after my vessel and fish with the same care as you do your watch." The skipper's ego collapsed like a burst balloon and the only fitting reply froze to his lips: if delivered it would suddenly have terminated his career as a skipper. Many skippers lacking the aplomb and fortitude necessary when sorely provoked, later bitterly rued having clashed with that owner.

One trawler, homeward bound, on its last section of the run home, encountered dense fog, radioed its owners, and reported having to reduce speed drastically accordingly. Feeling and groping its way down the Scottish East coast, before radar was thought of, the skipper had a reply, "Proceed with all speed for Monday's market". Unfortunately, he allowed his own better judgement to be over-ruled, resulting in colliding with and cutting a smallish coaster in half, and in some loss of life. Naturally, the Board of Trade blamed the whole sad happening on the skipper involved. Whatever happened to a vessel, the skipper was always held responsible – was he not in command? – Yet to exercise his full rights could bring down on his head repercussions leading to dismissal and the loss of his livelihood. About this time, in response to the pleas of many people of Hull, a commander of one of her Majesty's ships was sent to search for some trace of a trawler, the *St. Louis*, missing while bound for the Arctic, with my brother Leonard on board. On his return from the unsuccessful mission declared, "In those latitudes of eternal dark, such a quest was not feasible, an impossible task", and he could not understand why fishermen willingly chose to make their livelihoods in such waters. Personally, I could never understand why miners were so foolhardy as to venture down pits!

CHAPTER SIX

A return to Iceland is due here, and the bounteous harvest of the seas that surrounded its rocky, mountainous, volcanic coast. Fish were plentiful at various times in various places, of good quality and in many varieties which were in great demand on the home markets. The Icelandic Fjords provided havens for many ships in stress and storm, the hospitals and medical facilities ever ready for the stricken; there are even small cemeteries where fishermen, of several nationalities, are buried, having embarked on voyages never to return. Around the coast, dotted about the bottom of the sea, lie many ships, not all trawlers, with their crews. One such hapless vessel and probably the most illustrious, was the armed merchant cruiser HMS Rawalpindi sunk by enemy action on 23 November 1939. Twenty-four hours after hailing us through a megaphone and towering over us while baskets of fish were sent up her steep sides, she was engaged by the German battle cruisers *Scharnhorst* and *Gneisenau*, which were on their way to meet the pocket battleship the *Deutschland*. This was not a life or death struggle, but sure annihilation against the overwhelming, terrible might of the warships. The crew of the luckless vessel fought to the last while her huge bulk was blasted apart. With flag flying and all her eight-inch guns blazing, she sank below the waves to her final resting place off the East coast of Iceland. 238 valiant men died in this gallant and heroic action, including the Captain E C Kennedy; of the 48 men rescued, 37 were taken aboard by the German ships. The remaining 11 men were rescued by the HMS Chitral. Oh that we had been within sight or sound of the action, we could not have failed or even hesitated to fire a shot with our twelve-pounder in support. To have gone down fighting in her company would have been an honourable and glorious end. Several years later I read that one of the commanders of the German vessel was not proud of the savage onslaught that day. Well, we live and learn, but realization and wisdom are gained at no little cost, and far too late.

We ourselves had a brush with the *Deutschland*: some time after this action the German vessel suddenly loomed out of a bank of fog and almost capsized us by the tremendous bow waves as it passed close by, at very high speed, on its successful dash home to escape the revenge of the pursuing ships of the Royal Navy.

The fishing grounds on the West side of Iceland in particular were notorious for the loss and heavy wear and tear to the fishing gear. Hundreds of trawls and nets have been lost in the course of fishing there. To be able to work certain grounds needed much hard gained experience and costly, often heartbreaking times of trial and error. As long as fish consistently and contrarily inhabit rocky areas of the seabed, this will always be a bugbear and misfortune to the fisherman.

Some successful skippers had a habit of taking trips off during the slack time of year when catches were hard to come by. On one occasion our regular master was relieved by a young skipper while he had a holiday, and the locum had us away to Iceland for a trip, which could prove difficult for the inexperienced. After the first two or three days fishing, results were almost nil, heartbreaking in fact. The crew were becoming frustrated with working for nothing and so was the skipper who, in a fit of temper, threw a handful of coins into the sea loudly declaiming "I'll buy the fish if the powers that be begrudged me some".

The crew began voicing their displeasure after hauling the trawl once again for practically nothing (we were not catching enough to keep the galley supplied, and even the cook was becoming vociferous at the delay in filling his huge pan). The unfortunate skipper leaned out of the wheelhouse and said, "If anyone thinks they can do better, come up here." One chap immediately climbed the ladder to the bridge and took up the challenge. The skipper despondently inquired, "Where do you want the ship taken?" He directed the skipper to a position about forty miles away. The skipper then told him to take the wheel, gave him the compass course to steer and to ring the telegraph to stop the engines after four hours full steam. He then left him to it and took refuge in his bunk.

In due course we arrived at the new spot and recommenced fishing; when we hauled the trawl, we were all overjoyed at the changed result, a good catch which continued with every haul for several days. Had we fouled up the net, lost it on rocks or even had a poor result I would not have cared to have stood inside the sea boots of the man who had taken up the skipper's challenge. When we eventually landed our catch it sold well and on settling at the office, the skipper handed the challenger some bank notes and told him he was sacked. However, the returning skipper reinstated him.

On just another routine fishing trip to Iceland, the gale that interrupted our fishing operations was just another regular uncomfortable hazard most often encountered during the winter months. The vessel was hove to, buffeted and pounded, seas smashing aboard, wallowing into deep troughs, climbing steeply to plunge violently downwards, shuddering and staggering, reeling from blow after blow.

Groping along the deck towards the wheelhouse I was suddenly engulfed in a wall of water thundering on board, flung upwards and carried along in a mass of foam. Choking and fighting for breath I found myself several yards to the leeward of the vessel in a fairly calm patch of sea sheltered by the vessel laid with floodlights shining down on its decks and casting reflections into my darkness, as the vessel rolled, some deck debris floated near. I grabbed and held on to a deck board. The water was icy cold.

Encumbered by oilskins and thick woollen clothing, my sea boots holding water and dragging me down, I managed to kick them off and struggled to close the gap between the vessel and myself. The gap lessened when the vessel was pushed towards me by the seas only to open out as I drifted away. I yelled and swam. Had I been seen? Would I get back? The cold was stiffening my limbs. I could no longer feel anything but was terribly, frighteningly cold. About to give up hope and sink into merciful oblivion I heard shouts, lines were thrown and I was hauled back on board.

Later I learned that I had not been overboard for long but to me it was an eternity, there and then I decided to swallow the anchor and not tempt fate again. Alas, suitable jobs for fishermen ashore were non-existent and there was always the irresistible, magnetic pull of the sea, a powerful force from whose influence, once in its grip, only death could bring complete release.

"He sinks into thy depths with bubbling groan,
Without a grave, unknelled, uncoffined, and unknown". (Byron).

Cape Argona: Ernest served as boatswain between 1938 and 1939

CHAPTER SEVEN

Early in the Spring, the Polar ice began to crack and break away in parts from the main mass as a thaw set in, becoming a menace to all shipping in those waters, even at Iceland. In one of several similar happenings, a number of trawlers of Hull, Grimsby and a few German ones were fairly snugly lying at anchor in Isa Fjord on the North West coast of Iceland, sheltering from strong winds and rough seas when there was a sudden panic amongst the crews. Anchors were hurriedly weighed as icebergs were sighted sailing into the Fjord like tall ships under full sail. It was every ship for itself, to break out into the open sea to avoid being trapped or worse, but on reaching open water, we were not out of the wood: we found that even at our full speed of ten to twelve knots we failed to out-run the speeding masses of ice, and several vessels were soon in trouble when overtaken by it. Crunching and grinding our passage through the thinner ice flows, leaving behind a trail of red lead paint from the ships bottom, we fended growlers (huge chunks of ice) away from the propeller with long poles. Sometimes when trapped, we were carried along in the ice like a toy boat until the ice cracked, split apart and the powerful grip was released.

To digress, it is strange but true that there are occasions when one is safer at sea than in harbour. Two examples spring to mind, one during World War II when we left harbour for room to manoeuvre effectively in a bombing raid, and again when ordered out of the harbour at Mauritius on the approach of a cyclone.

"When stately ships are twirled and spun
like whipping tops and help there's none
and mighty ships ten thousand ton
Go down like lumps of lead" (R. Hodgson).

One Arctic wintry night in falling snow a sister ship, *Cape Spartel*, went aground whilst groping its way into Dyra Fjord. The rocky ground had holed the vessel and the crew launched their lifeboat, rowed up the fjord and boarded us in the *Cape Melville* riding at anchor. At dawn we tried to salvage the vessel. The Icelandic gunboat came on the scene, but despite our combined towage efforts we only succeeded in enlarging the holes in her bottom and pulling the vessel over on its side. By using the lifeboat as a ferry, we transferred 4000 stones of fish from her fish rooms and repacked in ice into ours. It involved a lot of hard work and effort, but as the fish had been under water all the night it was practically un-sellable when we returned to Hull. The Gunboat was awarded a fair sum for its salvage work but the crew preferred to let their hospitals have the money.

On one trip, after sheltering from bad weather for two days in Patreks Fjord, we steamed out to resume fishing operations. We proceeded three miles off the headland, stopped and dropped a dahn buoy to mark what at that time was the international fishing limit, and also to provide a mark to trawl by. Giving a sweeping illegal tow inside the buoy gave good results but on one such tow we observed smoke on the horizon. It was the gunboat, and by the time it drew near we were towing peacefully, well on the correct side of the buoy. Twice the gunboat steamed and measured the distance the buoy was off the land, and then seemingly satisfied she steamed out of sight round a headland. However, we were not fooled: a wisp of smoke could be seen stationary above the headland. After a day of cat and mouse tactics, the gunboat came along and approached us, and her captain bellowed through a megaphone, "Skipper, pick your buoy up and get to hell from here or I'll run you in Reykjavik."

It would have been folly to disregard this fair warning. On a similar occasion in 1930, we were not so lucky: when caught on the hop in the same spot, it cost us a £1900 fine and the loss of our catch and fishing gear which had to be bought back in order to carry on fishing. With the advent of the radio, the whereabouts of the few fishery protection boats was generally known, though to combat this patrolling aircraft and disguised fishing boats were brought into operation. There were good pickings to be had inside the limits at various spots around the coast. The conduct of the patrol boats was, in my experience, of the highest standards even though at times they were sorely provoked. Yet their assistance was always readily offered when required.

When fish was plentiful, we often toiled on deck for over thirty-six hours on end, leaving it only at meal times for half an hour at a time. The fish had to be gutted, washed and packed below in layers of ice. When we did get below, it was for four hours when we tumbled into our bunks fully clothed and slept like logs.

One outstanding trip was made in the *Cape Melville* about 1930; it was a record one to Iceland from Hull. We were three days on passage there; three days intensive fishing during which time over 2,000 ten stone kits of fish, all cod, were packed below, filling our fish rooms; then three days homeward bound, making just over nine days dock to dock. Our decks were not clear of fish when we sighted Scotland. Our expenses were under £400 and our catch realised about £1100.

One year as Christmas drew near, my kin persuaded me to leave my ship, the *Cape Dumer*, and stay home over the holiday. Many fishermen did this though neither the owners nor the trade cared for the ensuing disruption of fishing. However, I had spent many year ends at sea and decided to do as requested, knowing full well that after the holiday I would find it difficult to sign on again. Never-the-less, *Cape Dumer* sailed with a scratch crew, never to return: she was posted lost with all hands.

Trawlers that were to be away over Christmas carried a fair amount of Christmas fare, including legs of pork or a couple of geese, and most vessels, if fishing, laid for a few hours on the day. If the weather was good, it was not always good policy to cease fishing and lose a day in case the next day brought bad weather.

Long distance trawlers always carried bonded stores but these were strictly rationed, especially spirits, and we were often down to rolling fags from tea leaves, (which were less strong than old tarry rope on long trips).

There were no 'sirs' on board. Crews stood by a certain undefined, customary standard of discipline, recognizing that it was necessary and beneficial to all, but there were occasions when tempers overruled good judgement. One example was when a young, hot-headed mate dashed down a forecastle to shake up a hesitant crew, and was so shaken up himself, he had to be landed at the nearest port of call on a stretcher. Such incidents were, of course, exceptional.

All the crew from the skipper downwards were known chiefly by their surnames; but a few objected, saying they had been given handles to their names; many had well known, or well earned, nick-names, such as Truthful George who was anything but, Iceland John, Treacle Bob, Fairy Webb, Silent Chris, Jack the Bastard and so on.

The crews were good to all sea-birds; many men believed that when they left this world they came back as sea birds. Re-incarnation, what a glorious belief amongst fishermen. When they perched on the ships rails watching us work or strutted round the decks, we addressed them by the name of some ex-fisherman to whom they bore a resemblance in looks or appearance. They loved fish livers and would take them from our fingers or plead and beg for them. Fair weather or foul, wherever we ventured, they were our constant companions.

"It's a warm wind, the west wind, full of birds' cries." (John Masefield).

We envied the birds their freedom, their seemingly super-natural powers to endure and overcome the tremendous forces of nature. It sometimes seemed that the Arctic birds were indeed the spirits of long dead fishermen.

"They that go down to the sea in ships,
that do business in great waters,

These see the works of the Lord
And his wonders in the deep" (Psalm 107)

On board ship, recreation facilities were practically nil; cards, dominoes and reading were the main pastimes. As there was generally a watch below in their bunks, noise had to be kept to a minimum.

Crew changes in port were frequent. The average duration of a trip to distant waters was three weeks, with thirty six hours in dock between trips, and part of that time had to be spent at the offices on the dock. This routine could get tiresome over a few months and in order to have a little time on shore, one used to sign off and join another ship when ready to go back to sea, usually when spent up. In the short spell between trips, crews generally had sufficient earnings to live it up, and most were partial to drink, to "wash salt water out of their systems."

"The ship's clock in the bar says half past eleven.
Half past eleven is opening time.
The hands of the clock have stayed still at half past eleven for fifty years.
It is always opening time in the Sailors' Arms" (Dylan Thomas)

Like any big port Hull had a surplus of pubs, and quite a number of good time girls to be found in them. They knew most of the young seafarers who were free and easy, out to make full use of their time ashore, and they certainly did that. Parties went on all day and overnight. There was always the thought in the back of ones mind that the next trip or the one after could be the last one, as indeed it was for some, so why not make the most of the present.

"Oh how many sailors, how many captains,
who have gaily set out for long voyages
have vanished behind that sad horizon." (Victor Hugo)

Some hired a car and driver for shopping, a run up the coast or perhaps a race meeting or just to get about. At night they would generally meet up in the Tivali, the popular music hall.

CHAPTER EIGHT

On passage to and from the fishing grounds, we had plenty of time below, free and easy, taking watches, spells at the wheel and on lookout; we passed the watches away swapping yarns. In the dark hours there was only a tiny well-shaded light above the compass, which partly illuminated the helmsman.

The sunrises and sunsets we observed in every tiny detail and in every phase of change. They could be peaceful, in glorious tints of multi-coloured pastels, silver and gold, they could also be awe-inspiring when the skies were violently disturbed, a mass of dark, sombre, threatening clouds would clash with the most brilliant colours imaginable and a battle for supremacy raged over the whole sky, as with the 'Aurora Borealis' when the lights in the skies are reflected on the polar ice.

No one reads the portents of the skies as fishermen do, as their livelihood and well being, their very existence are akin to it. Sometimes the changes were so gradual and slow, as to be scarcely perceptible, or they could be sudden and dramatic.

"The sun's rim dips,
The stars rush out,
At one stride comes the dark." (Burns)

On one trip, in the face of a rising storm, the whole crew asked the skipper to stop fishing, but he refused. For us to disobey an order was mutiny and meant being logged with the consequent prosecution and court case on arriving back home. When hauling the trawl time came round, we all donned life jackets and roped ourselves together before venturing on deck. The skipper, taken aback, said "All right, get it aboard and lash it up."

It was not so easy on another occasion when a crew refused to shoot the trawl after several unsuccessful attempts to get it overboard, each time it was washed back again. The men were all logged and eventually appeared in court. How could the court, with all due respect, have any idea of the appalling weather conditions on that day which caused a decent hard working crew to throw in their hands so decisively? Such a refusal happened so rarely. To be overwhelmed in a rough sea with the gear down, acting as an anchor, is a terrifying and perilous ordeal. In some cases the gear has to be chopped away and lost.

Trawlers were exceptionally good seaworthy craft provided wind and seas were kept forward of the beam; with the weather on the quarter or astern they were vulnerable. They were ketch rigged with low bulwarks to discharge themselves quickly of waterlogged decks, and to enable trawls to be shot and hauled inboard easily. When well battened down they could plough through enormous seas, rear up and shake themselves clear before the next dive. Built like a Royal National Lifeboat, and not much larger at one time, the antics and acrobatics they could perform were unbelievable, except to those who sailed in them. They were able to list over until the side lights dipped in the water and just as quickly spring up and right themselves. On one ship, the cabin stove below decks came adrift, shot up a ladder through a doorway, and over the side, it was incredible, as if Neptune had reached inboard and appropriated it. Only a corkscrew motion could have caused its disappearance.

On another occasion, one of too many such, with a gale imminent, when hauling the nets in difficult conditions, the order from the bridge was "Just one more tow lads". To dispute the order was to invite trouble, to comply meant trouble, we were between the devil and the deep blue sea, with the greed for gold gaining the upper hand. That order should be classed amongst famous last words for trawler men, as to sneak in tow in a rising gale too often meant trouble all round. After a short tow came the inevitable cry, "Scramble the gear in lads" and scrambled aboard it was in a desperate struggle in gale force winds and heaving seas. Working furiously in waist high rushing water, odd chains were got round the gear to hold it in to the bulwarks in places, the loose net tangled in the scuppers, blocking escape holes and doors, now every sea that came aboard stayed there until rail high it slopped overboard.

"Look out" came a cry from the bridge, we dashed for cover or something solid to hang on to as a towering sea reared down to engulf us: the thud as it smashed into the structure was deafening. Down and over the vessel subsided under this terrific onslaught and tremendous weight of water, men floated outboard and back again as the sorely stricken vessel slowly surfaced, laid over with its port lights in the water. One more like that would have delivered the 'Coup de grâce'. Fortunately nearby vessels responded quickly to our radio call for aid and they formed an effective breakwater against the seas.

In response to frantic calls by the chief engineer, it was all hands down below to the bunkers, about fifty tons of coal had been jumped from the port side to the starboard side over the tunnel that ran through the bunkers to the fish rooms. As we toiled with our shovels the ship lay on her beam ends, in her crippled state it was impossible to hold her head up into the menacing seas. Our hearts really sank into our boots when the water cascaded through the engine room skylights, fused the lights at the switchboard and stopped the dynamo.

We laboured desperately, thrown and tossed about with just a faint glimmer of light from the boiler fires, until the coal was finally levelled. There was still a decided list, the cause of which was traced to be under the forecastle, where the heavy, neatly stowed anchor cable had been flung up along the ships side. That, after a struggle, was put right and we gained the deck in time to see the last of our oil money, the cod liver barrels, which had been securely stowed, disappearing astern.

Buffeted and pounded, seas smashing aboard from all angles, wallowing into deep troughs then climbing upwards only to plunge violently down again, the vessel shuddered and staggered, reeling from blow after blow. Water rushed down the forecastle and men had to claw their way out. At some time the ship's lifeboat vanished. What a terrific beating the ship took that night, yet when with daybreak, came an easing of the gale, the damage to the vessel was not great.

Afterwards, thanking the skippers who came to our aid by radio and informing them that we were seaworthy again they were as relieved as we were. It was a little consoling to find that a sea had smashed through the starboard side wheelhouse windows, flooded the bridge and given the skipper a good shaking up. Our trip curtailed, essential repairs were carried out in the fjords before the final run home.

My financial reward for that Bear Isle trip, two guineas a week (totalling five pound) went on sea kit, with no oil money: Neptune had taken that. There was no profit on the catch to share out as expenses were just cleared, it could have been worse we could have settled in debt. It was the hardest earned fiver in my life.

CHAPTER NINE

By the spring of 1936, the whole area of the Barents Sea had been trawled and scoured by hundreds of trawlers of several nationalities, and it was already showing the effects as vessels now had to search around large areas in order to hunt down the shoals of cod. The "dip and fill days" were coming to an end.

On our return from one trip with only a moderate catch, our skipper was informed of the owners plans to try an exploratory voyage to the waters round Greenland. A few years earlier in 1930 Hellyer Bros., a leading Hull firm of trawler owners, purchased a cargo ship and fitted refrigeration in the large holds. This was at that time a risky innovation, as refrigerators were being developed and were not too reliable. The vessel, *Arctic Prince*, was equipped with over forty Norwegian line fishing boats of the Dory type, light flat bottomed craft used by cod fishers of Newfoundland and N America.

When fitted out the vessel sailed to Norway to pick up a good number of Norwegian line fishermen before heading for Greenland. On the fishing grounds each working day the boats were launched and manned by a crew of two men whose job was to line fish with large sized hooks for the shoals of huge halibut, that gigantic king of all flatfish, which were known to inhabit these waters which formed their kingdom. Large quantities were caught and hauled on board the parent ship where they were hung in rows in the holds and immediately frozen. The vessel stayed at this fishing ground for nearly six months, then returned to Norway to land the boats crews before heading home for Hull.

Only a limited quantity of halibut was landed each day on the fish market to avoid any surplus supplies, and to keep the market price steady. The demand for such quality fish was good. A good class fish restaurant opened in the town, The Gainsbrough, which served only halibut steaks, it was highly successful, and indeed many fishermen queued to get in.

It took about three months to unload, a further three months to refit for another voyage. At Greenland ice and fog made it difficult to keep close contact with the boats when fishing. Also, as most of the boats had small engines that ran on methylated spirits, it was alleged at the time that many linesmen unwisely imbibed some of this and slept, letting their boats drift considerable distances. Whatever the reasons (profitability would have been the main one, not the fact that men's lives were at stake; life was cheap in those days) the whole of this fishing enterprise was given up and not attempted again. The same firm had plans to fly their vessels' catches home by large sea-planes daily to market and another scheme to use a speedy ex-naval corvette to transport fish catches from the distant grounds, but these ideas never got off the ground. A few of their trawlers began salt cod fishing at Iceland, daily landing their cod ashore to cod farms in Armar Fjord where the fish was beheaded and split open, wind dried in the open air on drying racks, then salted. After two or three months fishing they would load up and sail for home. This venture was also abandoned after a period.

Salt cod fishing was carried on by several Icelandic owned vessels but they did the splitting and salting at sea, dumping tons of waste fish over-board. To trawl over a bank they had worked on resulted in a catch of stinking cod heads and bones, they were almost as bad as hauling aboard large whale-bones which bubbled on deck as the trapped gases escaped in the open air.

Off the East coast of Iceland giant sponges were trawled up, some the size of whales, they were a nuisance tangling the nets, and if handled at all they caused a stinging rash on the face and hands. They had to be chopped up into manageable pieces to get them overboard. On the West side at certain times of the year, jelly fish (sluthers, we called them) would set in: they were also a hazard, a real bugbear, for they stung unmercifully even when splashed by them. To get a load in the trawl would bring the vessel up standing and cause damage to the gear, and they were most difficult to remove from the nets.

Fortunately, the most dreaded object to bring to the surface was not found in these waters; I refer to the sunken mines from the two world wars which were most often encountered in the North Sea, the Norwegian Coast and North of Scotland, in that order. Once when trawling in the Norwegian Deeps, which was once a good place for that new rare fish the Hake, we knew that we had picked up something unusual; it was most certainly not a gold watch. The vessel began to tow heavily, the propeller thrashed the water, and the towing warps closed together where they cut through the water.

The weather was moderate as we commenced to haul the gear to the surface, the noisy steam winch working flat out, spurting jets of steam from the cylinders as the pistons took the strain, but it was all it could do just to turn round, that winch was dealing with its stiffest task yet. After some time the Otter boards broke the surface and were heaved up to hang in the gallows and chained, the warps disconnected from them and the rest of the gear hauled.

The trawl could not be sighted as yet it hung very heavily directly below us, however getting the quarter ropes to the winch we got the 'bosom', the lower part, over the rail and on the deck then secured it with chains as it threatened to pull back overboard taking us with it. With the aid of rope beckets got round the bellies of the trawl we heaved the net up foot by foot until the cod ends were sighted. To our horror there was not one horned mine, but two. There was enough explosive alongside to send us on a journey through space and put us into orbit. Hurriedly we lowered the cod ends well below the water and debated our next move; to chop away the nets would take time, better to shoot the trawl and tow it well astern until we had got rid of our unwanted catch.

Four hundred fathoms of warp, all we could carry on the winch drums, were paid away and a grisly tow began. Suddenly to our relief the vessel's speed increased and we began to tow normally, our heavy burden had gone. On hauling the gear we saw that the cod ends had gone, they had torn away, it was a 'good riddance' and a lucky escape for us.

Unexpected objects were trawled up at times, particularly in the North Sea. Large parts of aircraft became quite common, and also things that had formed part of ships deck cargoes and presumably washed overboard. One vessel netted a five ton motor lorry and another skipper a piano; thereafter he was known as Jack the Pianist. Once we hauled a bag of fish on board and the mate let go the cod-line, as the fish cascaded onto the deck the body of a dead seaman dropped out in such a way that one of its arms dropped round the surprised mates neck holding it in an upright position, despite his alarmed cries of "Git off" and "Let Go". Shipwrecks and old sailing ships anchors were the most troublesome and did the most damage to our gear.

DETAILS OF TRAWL NET AND BOARD

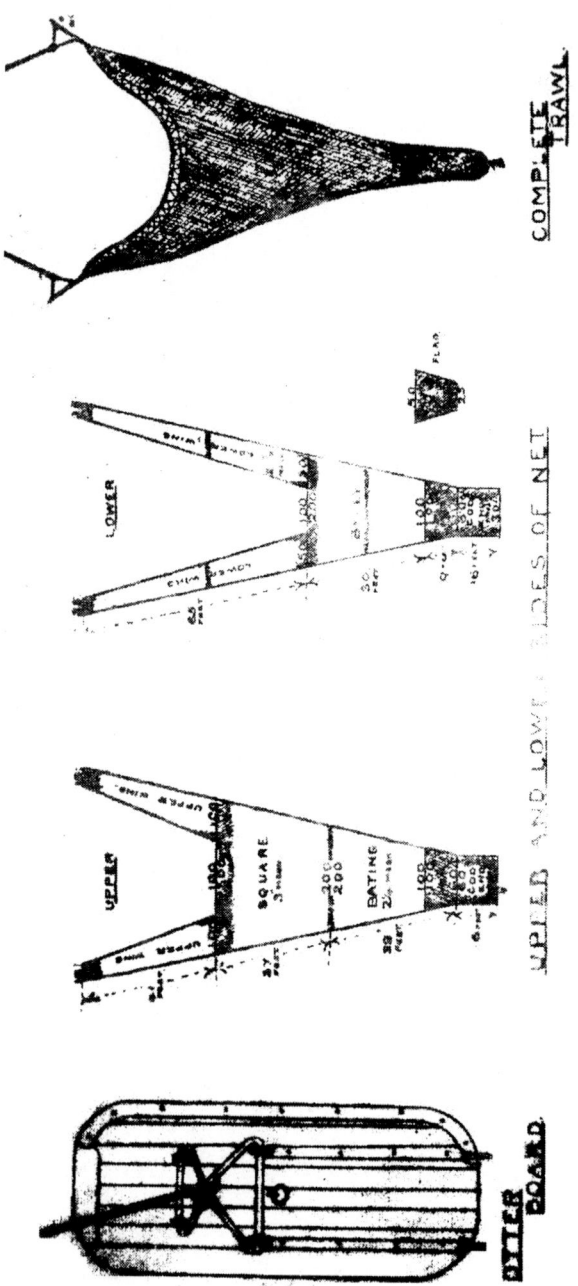

Trawl net and Board

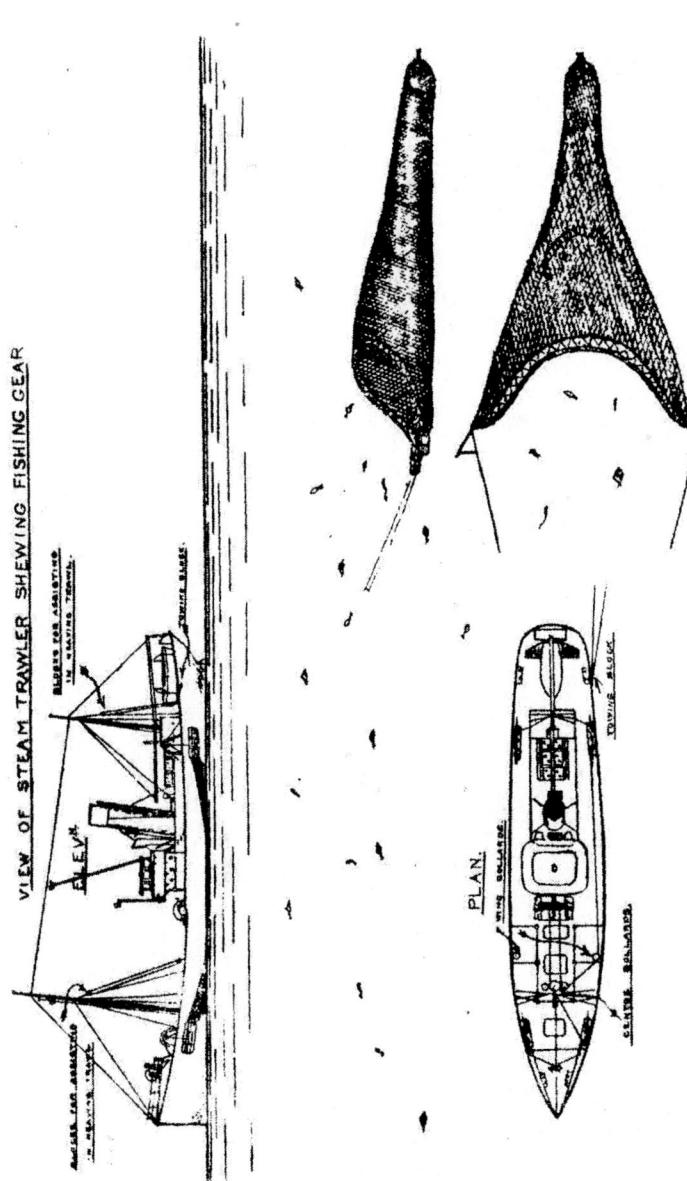

Trawlers Showing Fishing Gear

Nets

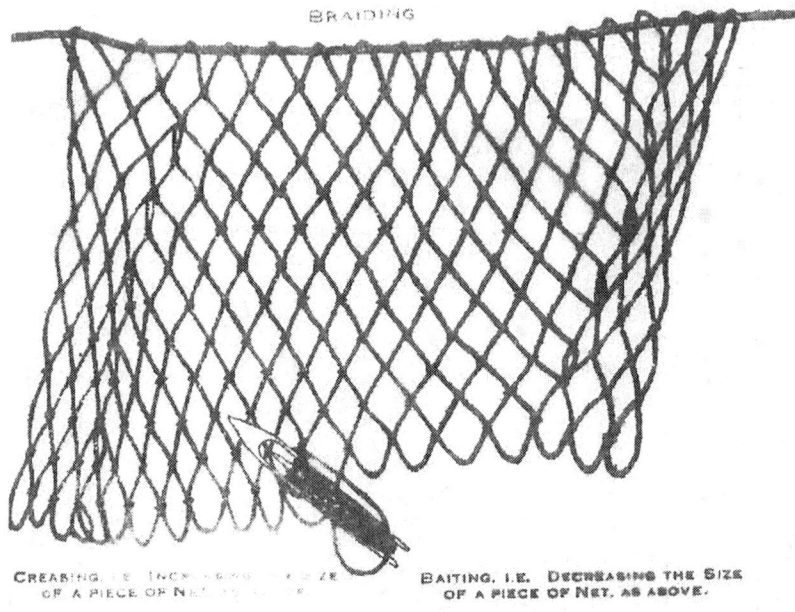

BRAIDING

CREASING, I.E. INCREASING THE SIZE OF A PIECE OF NET, AS ABOVE.

BAITING, I.E. DECREASING THE SIZE OF A PIECE OF NET, AS ABOVE.

COD END.

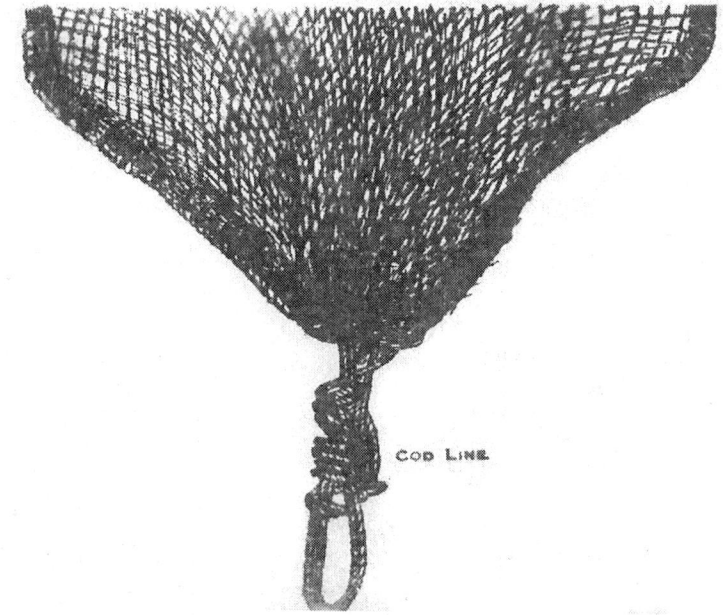

COD LINE.

Net Lines

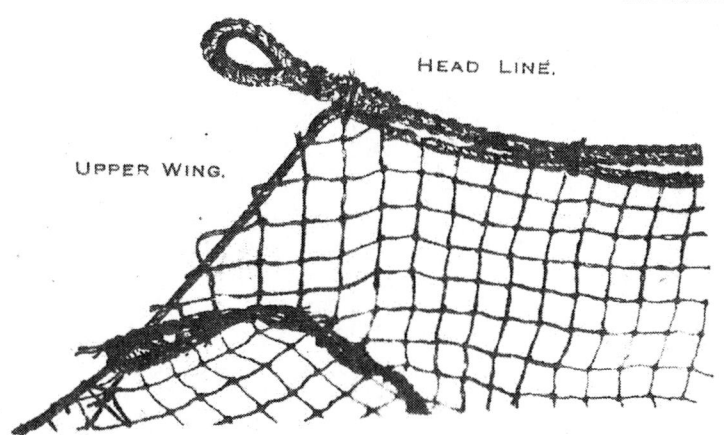

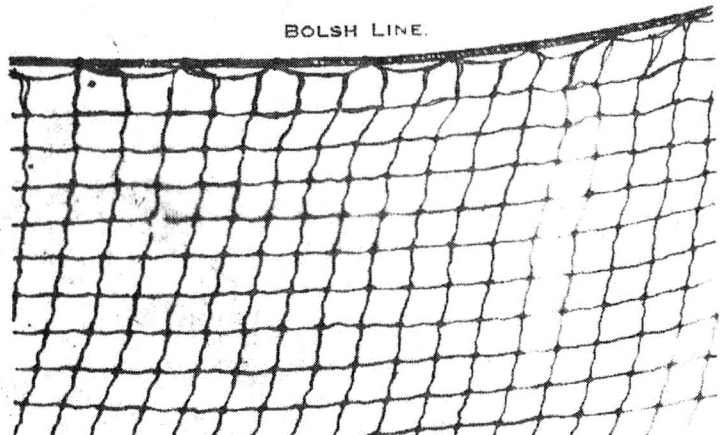

WHEN BOLSHING LOWER WINGS TAKE TWO FLYING MESHES EACH TIME AND NEVER LET THEM EXCEED THREE ORDINARY KNOTS

BOBBINS FOR USE WHEN WORKING ROUGH GROUND

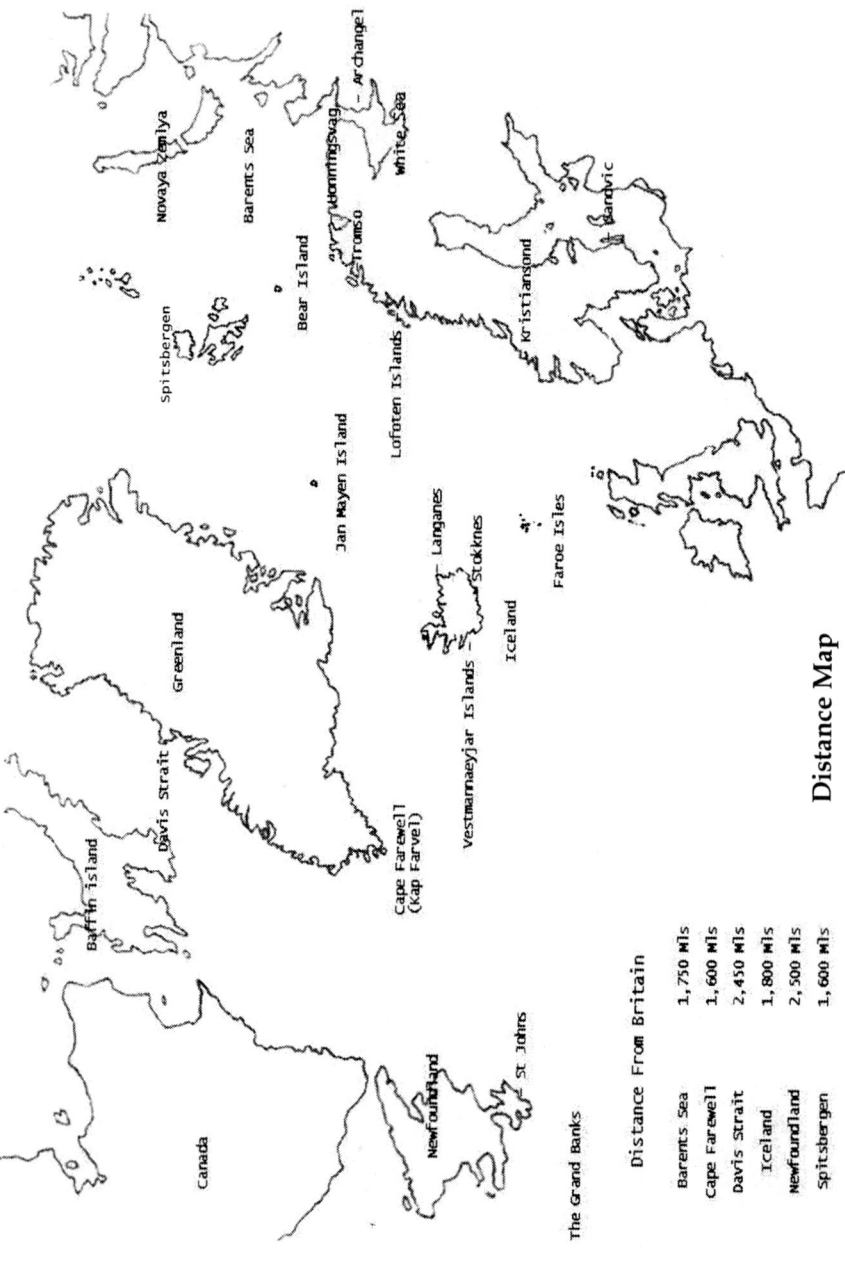

Funnel Markings Page 1

Hull Trawler Funnels

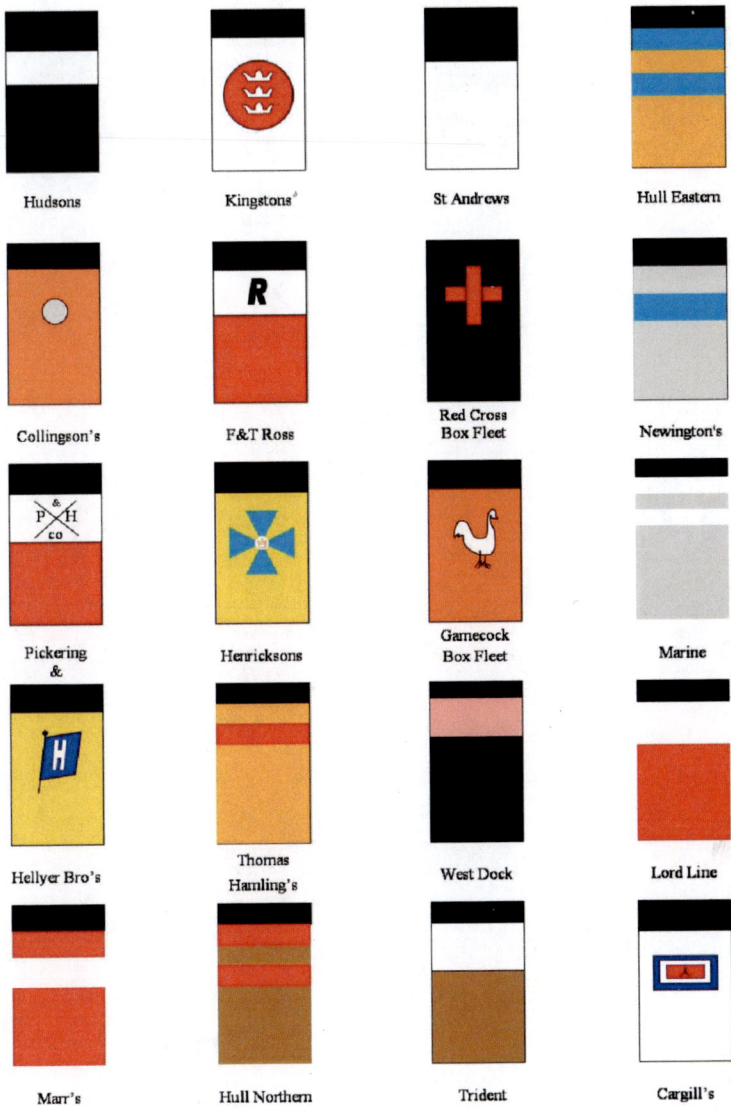

Funnel Markings Page 2

Hull Trawler Funnels

Oddson & co

K Percival & Co

Yorkshire Trawlers

Boston

Boyd Line

Charlston Smith

Eton

Northern

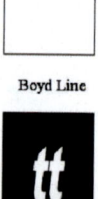
Hull Merchants Amal.

Lock Fishing Co

Ocean Steam Trading Co.

Victoria Fishing Co.

CHAPTER TEN

Greenland was a new venture, an unknown quantity, so it was not surprising when most of the crew signed off the ships log. However they were replaced (with some difficulty) but first we all had to pass the doctor's examination as there would be little chance of medical aid on this trip. The skipper asked me, as bosun, if I would stay with him; I replied "Why not? It can't be any worse than the rest of the Arctic". I was then introduced to a youngish Merchant Navy officer who was signing on as navigator, a requirement insisted upon by the vessels insurers. At that time, skippers had a Board of Trade Certificate of Competency gained on dead reckoning navigation, not great circle sailing. However, as sextants were practically useless where the sun and stars were seldom seen, a navigator was not really necessary, but he proved to be a popular and useful man about the ship. The sailing day was August 12th 1948 when we left Hull for the new grounds.

Our departure point for Cape Farewell in Greenland was Cape Wrath, on the northern tip of Scotland. We had logged over two thousand miles when we first shot our trawl in a position well up the East coast. After several unsuccessful attempts to get a clear tow in on a few grounds, we only succeeded in hauling torn nets and huge clumps of submerged undergrowth. Our operations were then switched to the Western side where first results were promising.

The further North we ventured the denser and more prolific were the shoals of cod. When, about six hundred miles up the coast, we found that we were unable to proceed further; to our surprise we discovered that our compasses had stopped swinging freely and were getting sluggish and unreliable. The compass cards bearing the needles were being drawn downwards by a magnetic force until they rested on the bottom of the bowl and were almost vertical. This phenomenon was no doubt due to our proximity to the magnetic pole.

We commenced to fish in earnest surrounded by miles of slushy ice and in the space of three busy days our fish rooms were full: we had hauled on board well over two thousand ten stone kits of cod with quite a large number of halibut. At full speed we headed south; our trip was by no means over, there was still the catch to get to market in good condition, nine days and nights of continuous steaming in favourable weather, but getting clear of Greenland was to prove a nightmare.

After travelling through miles of pancake ice, flat ice flows with curled up edges through constant nudging together, resulting in the wonderful appearance of giant water lilies, we ran into growlers, huge chunks of ice that had broken away from the main mass. They could be dangerous, as two thirds of their bulk was out of sight and could be drawn into the suction of the propeller. Towards midnight as we were making some headway, the weather changed abruptly, a terrible spine-chilling freezing coldness embraced us and we soon knew from whence it came: Icebergs. Some were like floating islands, others just a towering mass of solid ice as we found ourselves in their midst. Due South was where we wanted to be, but according to the drift of the ice, South West was the wisest course and it was all hands on watch to remain so for the rest of that night. Keeping a lookout from the bows and from all parts of the ship, yelling sightings of ice to the bridge we manoeuvred a passage through the moving ice that threatened to reduce us to a heap of scrap iron. Bergs mast high crashed like cracks of thunder as they collided and tore each other apart. Some bounced past and capsized, turning turtle and sending out huge waves from the backwash. The rising wind howled ferociously, shrieking through the bergs and around them, forcing them to move along in utter confusion. It was the wind against the solid ice, there was not sufficient open sea for it to rise to the winds bidding, none-the-less, there was a very angry disturbed sea. To add to our predicament, clouds of snow enveloped us, blown from the surface of the ice, at times reducing visibility to nil. We had to head away from the land due West when we discovered icebergs were running aground along the coast even as far off as the fifty fathom line which meant that they had a depth of over three hundred feet below the water, but, at a standstill they could be avoided if seen in time. Fortunately, as our bows reared upwards and plunged down, waves were pushed outwards causing the bergs directly in our path to swerve and pass along our length. The faint light from the stars was reflected on the ice with a glow that only emeralds possess, and the dark crevasses emphasized the contrast.

The picture was taken from the vessel's rail when trawling off the North Cape of Iceland amongst the pancake ice flows. When rubbing together the edges curl up to appear like a sea of giant water lilies. The sun was just sufficient to cast the vessel's shadow onto the ice. Shortly after this peaceful picture was taken, the weather changed, the flows joined up and quickly became a solid, impenetrable barrier.

We were in a strange world, not entirely supernatural: our bleary eyes and numbed senses knew the vivid reality of our surroundings; they were not mystical nor flights of fancy. It was a lonely world and even the sea birds had deserted it.

"So lonely t'was, that God himself
Scarce seemed there to be". (Burns)

As the helm was spun this way and that, ice scraped the ship's hull and the more solid lumps struck and sheared off. We survived that night of 'all Hell let loose' but it was not until we had put over eighty miles behind us that the ice opened out and there came a little daylight and an easing of the wind: winds of such fury cannot last long. As to our position on the chart, that was anyone's guess, but it was up to the navigator to sort that one out. We must have been on the wrong side of the Davis Straits somewhere off Baffin Island. Seamen seem to be a rare breed: they endure a bitter fight for life against fearful odds and when the turmoil has passed, all is forgotten save for any humorous incident that is recalled that did not call for a laugh at the time it took place. At the height of the storm our young deckie-learner was sent on the veranda with an axe to chop the ice from around the bridge windows. Unable to distinguish which from which he put the axe through two windows. The infuriated skipper grabbed the axe and if he had caught up with the fleeing lad an execution would have taken place there and then. For the sorely taxed, overwrought skipper it must have been 'the last straw'.

First trippers to sea were greenhorns, and the butt of practical jokes: one might miss a new gutting knife and then on gutting his first cod, be amazed to find it inside the fish. The old hands of course would push these objects down a cod's throat into its gullet and place the fish so that the intended victim gutted it. Those rounded up and signed on for Christmas trips by 'hard up for men' ships runners, were known as 'Christmas Crackers'.

We landed two thousand three hundred ten-stone kits of firm well fed cod which sold readily enough and realized £2500. In those days if a catch of cod fetched an average of £1 per kit, it was a satisfactory trip. Our expenses were considerably higher than incurred by the trip to other grounds, about £900. We were paid a share of the sum after expenses had been deducted. The skipper drew £10 to the £100, the mate £7, the bosun four-pence and the common or garden deckie, two-pence. The engine room staff of four were also on a graduated scale. The navigator had been engaged at a salary of 7 guineas a week and for helping us out on deck we allowed him a share of the not inconsiderable sum of oil money obtained from the excellent cod livers. The hands' standing wage weekly was 2 guineas.

At Hull fish market the men who unloaded the trawlers were called 'bobbers'; they wore clogs and as they tramped down to the docks before 2 a.m. they roused the neighbourhood. Generally they were unloaded by the time the sales started around 7.30 a.m. especially about this time, 1936, when electric winches were installed on the market to greatly reduce the heavy manual power required of the men, of whom many were ex-fishermen. The same workers at nearby Grimsby were known as 'lumpers'. Also what became known as the 'filleting trade' was starting up which gradually boosted the price of cod, prior to this cod was considered a very inferior fish, certainly not one of the well known prime fish. Filleted fish readily obtainable also created an expansion in the popular fish and chips emporiums (as they were often called). Their best seller then were small haddock. There were three sizes of small 'ducks' – Nits, Ping Pongs and Chats, one could get 400 to 500 'Nit Haddocks' in a six stone basket and one skipper, 'Nitty Harland', earned his nick-name through catching so many in the North Sea. They were still good value coated with batter and fried, despite the bones: at two pence or three pence a piece according to size, with a penny-worth of chips, one had a feast for the Gods, they were a very tasty morsel indeed. For that outlay one could also help oneself generously to salt and vinegar and in the occasional saloon, a pickled onion to make the newspaper packet a banquet.

Though we had minor dints and dents above and below the water line, the top half of the stem set back a foot or so, and the hull scraped bare of paint, repairs were quickly completed and arrangements made for a second trip to Greenland. The navigator and I had got on so well together at sea that we spent the whole time in dock visiting pubs and clubs, imbibing freely on a prolonged binge. There were a few crew changes, since some did not relish another trip to the same area, but after thirty six hours in dock, the normal time between trips, we were again on our way.

It was in the dark hours when we fetched Cape Farewell, and we laid until dawn before entering the ice fields and steaming up the coast. We were unable to distinguish between the coastline and the stranded ice-flows and bergs, but we discovered that keeping over thirty miles off there was much less ice to contend with. The weather had been squally since leaving Scotland and was still much the same. We ran into an extensive stretch of open water, appearing, because of the ice, rather like an inland sea, and we took soundings. It seemed a likely spot and so it proved: after fifteen minutes tow the warps closed and it was time to haul up. Before the trawl doors were hung up the cod ends rose and lifted clear of the sea, slowly the bellies floated and the whole trawl was full of nice plump cod. Most round fish drew in air whilst being hauled to the surface causing the net to float; other fish (especially flat fish) were difficult to deal with, they were just dead weight, and a good catch would often tear the nets away. Cod were by far the easiest and best fish to handle quite apart from the excellent livers they provided, and in the spring when they were spawning, each female cod contained perfect roes consisting of an average of nine million eggs. I leave it to the reader to work out how many eggs would be in a ten stone kit of roes, or if one pair of roes is purchased for a delectable meal how many 'could have been' cod they have consumed. After spawning, cod were still in pretty good shape, unlike herrings, haddock and salmon: they became nothing but skin and bone, razor-backs, as they were known in the trade.

When a cod end, or bag, was hoisted inboard, the codline holding the bottom together was released by the bosun, as a slip knot is, and the fish then cascaded over the deck which was divided into squares or pounds with boards, to contain the fish and to prevent it moving. Fishermen wading waist high, the fish was then gutted, sorted and tossed over the hatches into the washing pounds on the opposite side, and thoroughly hosed before being taken below and buried in ice crystals. A good crew could deal with around seven hundred kit a day, working day and night with little time off the deck. Years later washing machines were used to speed the process.

On the cod

Torn nets were a bugbear at any time but in these climes they meant extreme hardship when either mending or replacing them, and were the cause of many frost bitten fingers. In general, the areas favoured and frequented by the cod shoals, were good towing grounds as they were in the North Sea. As to clothing, we wore woollen underwear, fear-noughts (trousers of woollen cloth), two ganseys (Guernseys), sea boots and two pairs of sea boot stockings. Oil-skins were worn much of the time, not only to keep us dry, as they provided the best protection against the bitterly cold winds. If a man was unfortunate and went overboard either the freezing water would instantly stop his heart, or the weight of his clothes would drag him down deep out of sight, a quick end it was comforting to know.

It was little wonder that many accidents occurred when fishing: slippery decks, a rolling ship, wire warps being run out or heaved in, working round a winch with its moving parts fully exposed, wires and ropes that often parted, and heaving great weights on board, all apart from what the sea could inflict. On the second day's fishing, a deck-hand sustained a crushed arm in hauling. Needing medical help we made for Godthaab, which was frozen up during the winter months to all shipping, a smallish settlement of Danish people living in wooden houses with rather primitive sanitation (Godthaab's inhabitants being inclined to visit the slopes of the nearby snowy ridges). Getting out of our little private sea proved difficult: the ice surrounding it had, unknown to us, thickened considerably, and had we stayed much longer the services of an ice-breaker would have been required. As the stem cut into the ice it cracked and split open for some way ahead but now and again the ship almost stopped, the bows would rise a foot or so over the ice and the weight of the vessel would take it down through it.

In port the man's arm was attended to but for the rest of the trip he would be a passenger. Fishing was resumed about a hundred miles further south in the most extraordinary brilliant sunshine and the reflection from the floating ice was dazzling. The sea was so blue, truly a royal blue which contrasted vividly with the glittering diamond whiteness of the ice. This was storm swept ice, battered, scoured and windswept, carved by the forces of nature into the most intricate, delicate shapes and forms of art, the picture gradually changing as the royal procession slowly, majestically moved southwards, fearlessly, in a stately manner, to their complete destruction in the warmer climes. It would not have surprised us to see, in fact we were disappointed not to have seen, a sculptured king of this domain on a throne of ice come gliding by, it was so enchanting.

The complete silence and the stillness of the air was suddenly disturbed by the clatter of the winch, the thud of the engines, the thrashing of the propeller, the shouts of the men, all were magnified out of all proportion. We missed our friends, the seagulls, Kittys, Mollys and Gannets, their screeching and their cheeky thieving from our catches; it was so curious their absence in this area, perhaps they had more sense than we.

Apprehensively, knowing how quickly all this tranquillity could change, the fishing continued unceasingly: it was surprising how monotonous the job could become. It was, in the main, exhausting, heavy, manual work. Even for the skipper there was little relaxation: from the commencement of fishing to the finish some skippers never left the bridge, having their meals brought to them and snoozing in a corner when possible, this could go on for several days. In daylight the ice was no trouble to us, but in the dark hours the extreme cold warned us of the presence of bergs in the vicinity. When near to them, a rough distance could sometimes be estimated by timing the distance between blows of the fog horn and hearing its echo. If blown for a similar reason when entering a fjord in falling snow or fog, echo after echo would resound up and down the fjord and sometimes cause a small avalanche down the mountain sides.

At the end of the thirteenth day at sea, holds full, we were U.K. bound, able to clean ourselves up and enjoy a full watch below in the warmth and comfort of our bunks, taking the strain on all parts as it were. Our trip was again successful, but our fuel bill was heavy and Greenland was ruled out for future fishing. Our navigator, loath to leave, re-signed on as a member of the crew. After a twelve-month fishing he could then obtain a skippers ticket. In the 30's there was a disastrous slump in shipping, docks were full of laid up ships, and a number of big ship men became trawler men but very few stayed the course, finding it vastly different to what they were accustomed to in the Merchant Navy.

CHAPTER ELEVEN

The fishing community was a fairly close one; most of the folk lived in the South-western part of the city. Many of the men folk, when ashore, used the pubs and clubs in the area and those who had left the sea continued to mix with the sea-going. At the earliest age possible, sons followed fathers and grandfathers into fishing, so that many names were very well known. Earnings could be good over periods, a successful skipper's yearly income could compare with that of a Prime Minister at that time. Some were able to have their own vessels built and found firms of their own. Several were naturalized Danes, Norwegians or Icelanders. A few skippers had gained their tickets by the age of twenty one years - to accomplish this one had to obtain a 'ticket' which required four years at sea, time ashore was not counted - therefore this meant that they had started sea going around fifteen years of age.

In general, fishing families married between themselves as the womenfolk were accustomed to long frequent absences of the men while at sea. Sometimes if a man chose a wife unfamiliar with the fishing life it was not long before she began to plead persistently with her spouse to give up the sea. The knack and know-how of knitting heavy woollen ganseys, long boot stockings and underwear was handed down from one generation to the next. The womenfolk were inured to withstand tragedy and misfortune, to many it was part of their lives.

Near St. Andrews dock often called simply fish dock, there was a chapel known as the fishermen's bethel, whose pastor had the thankless duty of visiting and notifying families of a ship overdue or if misfortune had befallen anyone. Wives also had the task of bringing up their children in the absence of the father. Every Friday was the fish dock races, when the wives and families decked themselves out in their best and vied with each other with the latest model prams. It was the day the crew's wages were collected from whichever firm the men folk sailed for; if a deckhand, it would be two guineas, less stoppages. After the visit to the docks there was the parade into town and round the shops, it was quite a day out for many and a time of meeting friends. There would be little of the pay-out left at the end of the day but there was the next Friday to look forward to.

On fine days, looking down the streets of closely packed terraced spotlessly clean houses of the fisher folk, one would see groups of women comparing their babies or knitting away with large knitting needles. Around Easter time they would handle long ropes across the streets and skipping was the order of the day, twenty or thirty jumping as the rope came down; some had babes in their arms and even the men joined in. Their homes were open to anyone as they walked in and out of each others' place. All helped each other and when tragedy struck a family there was no lack of support and commiseration. Many women made parts of the trawl nets, working as fast with braiding needles as when knitting and long lengths of net would be trundled on to the deck in old prams and taken to the net making firms.

All women at that time wore aprons and shawls, but by the end of the 1920's the old ways of dressing died out in favour of modern dress, and the men's ganseys or white silk mufflers changed to collars and ties. The whole street would turn out for a wedding or a funeral. Any good excuse would call for a street party when pianos were dragged out into the street along with tables and chairs. The open air rabbit pie suppers with jugs of beer were not to be missed nor the 'knees up Mrs Brown' and equally popular dances that always followed on. Three of these streets were know as Faith, Hope and Charity, and when I went down one of these to visit my grandparents I had to run a gauntlet of looks and murmurings - anyone could tell who I was related to, whom I was on my way to visit, if I was looking well or no. Things were looking up if I wore something new, or it could just as obviously be otherwise; everything and everyone was their concern.

Religion was mainly the women's prerogative, the men seldom had the time or opportunity for it, but they were all too familiar with the:-

"Dark-heaving – boundless, endless and sublime,
The image of eternity, the throne
Of the invisible." (Byron)

As the winter months were again with us, Iceland was to be our next destination. It was strange; a few years earlier it had been the centre of all good fishing, but since the opening of fresh grounds elsewhere we had not fished its waters for at least two years, and we looked forward to renewing our acquaintanceship. Trawlers bound for Iceland and the Faroes battled their passage through the Pentland Firth that separates the Orkneys from the mainland and which is notorious for the powerful tides that sweep through the narrow straits. The older, lower-powered trawlers would lie outside and await a favourable tide; a vessel could be capable of ten knots and still make no headway against the current. During the daylight hours we would sound the ships whistle when under the snow-white lighthouses that towered above us, and the keepers wives would emerge from their, without question, spotless kitchens to wave a tea towel to bid us on our way. They welcomed our greeting as much as we did theirs, and never failed to respond. It was the last glimpse of a woman for a good spell; indeed for the unlucky; it proved to be the very last.

To digress, when on escort duty during the war, with a convoy from the Firth of Forth, our commodore had arranged before sailing for the Pentland Firth lighthouse to be lit at his E.T.A. (estimated time of arrival) for one hour. Owing to the weather deteriorating we arrived an hour late at Duncansby Head as the lighthouses were being blacked out. Within minutes, six large cargo ships were aground to keep the neighbouring R.N. Lifeboats busy for the rest of the night. The fast flowing tide was a problem when it joined forces with the rough seas. Halfway through, our decks were clean swept in a tidal wave which snatched our firmly secured depth charges from their racks over the stern. We emerged from the Firth into a gale and from then on it was every ship for herself. Fortunately in that weather the U-Boats were no threat, but threading a way through the unlit Minches, inside the Hebrides, down to Oban on a murky night was quite enough to try the patience of Job.

We did know the Icelandic area pretty well, the rough rocky grounds where trawls were easily crippled (we called them 'hospital cases'; this occurred all over the West side), but the cod banks on the East and South Sides were mainly good for trawling. There was also good fishing of various kinds around the dreaded Nord Kap (North Cape), but it was not a pleasant spot in the winter months. Iceland had advantages to offset the disadvantages: it afforded shelter from the elements, there were doctors and hospitals at hand, ship repairs could be done, or stores obtained. It was well endowed with lighthouses, but navigation round its coasts could be tricky in parts due to the localised attraction of the compass to the magnetic iron bearing rock, especially on the South coast; this needed to be guarded against when making a landfall. Particularly dangerous was Mount Hekla, still an active volcano that exerts a powerful magnetic influence to lure many ships ashore in the area. In most cases they were a total loss, as they were at the Ingolf's Hefde (the Hoof to us), their wrecked hulls adding to the existing magnetic attraction. When a shipwrecked crew did succeed in gaining the shore the local farmers helped them on the long arduous pony ride through the boggy land that lay ahead of them before reaching a settlement.

About fifty miles west of the North Cape the cod grounds were known as the 'Hindenburg Line'. Large German trawlers sometimes fished there, but the weather could be ferocious and, if caught out there, it was a long run to seek shelter. Two Icelandic-owned trawlers were lost with all hands in this area, and the crews' dependents appealed to the owners to stop sending their ships so far off the land; ironically, they now demand a two hundred mile limit for foreign vessels fishing these waters.

St. Andrews S.T.C. trawling nearby off the North Cape, Iceland. It is unusually clear of ice even for the summer months when icebergs travel to well south of this area. When the ice barrier reaches the Cape it cannot be rounded for the East side; a place to be dreaded for much of the year.

Generally, time spent on the fishing grounds could range from eight to fourteen days depending on the weather and results. The first few days we fished for flats and haddocks at several places along the west coast with a lot of net mending which always caused sore hands, especially in those days when nets and twines were of sisal dipped into a mixture of tar to preserve them. It was a big step forward in fishing when, in the 1950's, manufactured man-made fibres replaced the sisal and manila that had been used for centuries.

We shot off Isar Fjord on a well known cat-fish ground, this was a much disliked place to work, as a bag of large lively cats on the deck was more than a nuisance, struggling and fighting back when handled, and sinking their teeth into anything near at hand.

They had such a hard bony head a club was of little use to quieten them down. If one was picked up and put to a wire hawser, it would hang on to it and grind away with its teeth until it almost gnawed it through. To get in amongst them whilst they were still alive and strong was foolish as our sea boots would be ruined in their vicious teeth which were hinged, should a hand or fingers get in their mouths it was futile to pull back, it only tightened the grip. The only way to free oneself was to stab your knife into its eye and its mouth would open wide in pain or anger. It was then a generally accepted fact that fish, being cold blooded, did not feel pain, but the way some reacted to the touch of cold steel does not seem to bear this out. It is also widely believed that fish do not make audible sounds, but these cat-fish certainly contradicted that: they grunted, snapped and snarled. When gutted, we found they were full of ground up shells; perhaps acute indigestion was the root cause of their extreme display of bad temper.

Gale force winds interrupted our fishing here and we ran for the shelter of the fjord. On the way in our gear had to be unshackled from the warps and the net stowed, a necessity before entering the fishing limits to show compliance with the law at the time. We anchored well inside, under the lee of the snow capped mountains, 'snug as a bug in a rug'. The next morning at dawn an Icelandic patrol boat sent a boarding party across to us. After inspecting the gear an officer began to pull a few barely alive plaice from the meshes of the net and accused us of having trawled in the fjord during the dark hours. It seemed that the village men had set lines at dusk and apparently they had been towed away. Of course, some skippers were not above doing that sort of thing, but we were innocent. Despite our explanations that flat fish, particularly plaice, could keep alive in a cold wet spot for a few days, he left us muttering threats and extremely unsatisfied. Obviously he was neither an ex-fisherman, nor a gentleman – anything but in our opinion!

The same patrol boat party then boarded a vessel that had evaded a chase by a patrol boat on a previous trip, but found that the skipper they wanted had cunningly and wisely changed ships; it definitely was not that officer's day. A patrol boat could be very tenacious, in one instance a trawler was chased as far as the Orkneys before giving up after the patrol boat fired several rounds from its gun. Another Hull trawler was escorted into Reykjavik under arrest and two armed guards put aboard, who were plied with drink, and the vessel slipped away in the dark hours to reach home unmolested.

We left the sanctuary of the fjord and rounded the North Cape to complete our trip cod fishing down the east side. When working the edge of the banks, we occasionally trawled up a blue shark, or one of the breed of shark then called a Hawkettle. The blue sharks, of no use to us, were immediately dumped, but the Hawkettles, up to twenty feet in length, though a nuisance, were stripped of their huge juicy livers which filled a couple of six stone baskets, then a rope becket was got round the thick part of the tail, and it was hoisted mast high to allow us to swing the carcase outboard. It was then lowered and chopped through its tail end to avoid netting it a second time. One skipper earned the title of 'Hawkettle Jack' for the number he caught. It was strange that the larger the fish (or mammal) taken from the water, the quicker it expired on the deck, with the exception of the conger eel; these, even after gutting, (which no-one relished doing), and washing, would still be active. One old fisherman's tale was of a deck hand who laid one out as usual, in an empty pound down the fish room and covered it with ice, but each time he went to pack fish away, the eel was in full view, he resorted to more and more ice until the pound was half full with the eel still on top. Possible? Yes, very much so.

Approaching the south east coast on our run home, the watch notified the skipper that they could see the land. "Not yet", he replied, but on peering through the binoculars, he agreed it looked very much like it. On getting closer we were surprised to identify what at first appeared to be rocks with the surf lapping over them, but was actually a group of whales laid on the surface contentedly suckling their young, with their huge tails hard over like a ships rudder, to hold their heads up into the current to counteract drift. To get a better view of such a rare, wonderful, dramatic event and not wishing to disturb them in any way, we edged nearer and were soon convinced that we were intruding on a very intimate time of their lives, their giving birth. Slowly we turned away leaving them to their privacy. Not until after we had lost sight of them did we see the land, so they must have been well offshore.

Whilst steaming down the Scottish coast I took over a watch and found our now ex navigator with his binoculars riveted on the shore. "Can you see a woman?" I joked, and his reply shook me profoundly, it was a remarkably keen, perceptive observation that had never occurred to me before, "I can see a tree; in all our travels in the Arctic, I never see a single tree, from leaving home to arriving back."

Trawlers, when launched, were christened with a bottle of wine and as much ceremony as an ocean going liner. Their economical speed was ten knots, and if a coal-burner, this used about ten tons a day, if the vessel was pushed this could rise to fourteen tons.

There were the currents and tides to allow for, also the weather. Most Hull trawlers were locally built, those known as the three B's 'Beverley built bastards' (no discredit or reflection on the builders), the chief reason was that they were so lively at sea, unshipping everyone and everything, whereas the Goole boats were the opposite, preferring to go through a sea rather than over it, hence they were 'bloody dreadnoughts', but all vessels had their own individual peculiar ways at sea, very unpredictable and aptly referred to as she or it in polite conversation. To fishermen, they were anything but 'a lady'; albeit, they were the most seaworthy ships afloat when they were in fair trim. When down by the head, crippled, with the dead weight of fish or fuel, or high up in the water in a balloon-like condition, their behaviour was incredible. The life of a trawler generally depended on the life of the boiler, which could be a good twenty years, and many went very much longer. To replace a boiler, the vessel had to be almost torn apart.

CHAPTER TWELVE

Most crews generally favoured voyages to the White Sea except in mid winter when much of that area was frozen over and the timber carriers could not reach Archangel until the spring. These trips gave us a nice break from the ordinary routine, with journeys through some of the most wonderful inland water-ways in the world. Very occasionally, and only if the weather was really bad, we would make for Kristiansund to commence about a thousand mile cruise between the chain of outer islands and the mainland with a local pilot on board. During the summer months, the constantly changing magnificent scenery held one spell-bound. Snow capped mountains towered on either side, dotted with pines on the lower slopes and with every few miles a picturesque settlement or village nestled at the foot of them near the waters edge, all made up a spectacular panorama. The channels were so narrow in places, vessels could not pass each other, but the blue water was incredibly deep, even where the mountains rose steeply from its depth. Steaming along, it seemed in many places we were in a cul-de-sac, hemmed in on all sides, yet the land slowly unfolded as we moved onwards. Many small ferries travelled to and fro, their decks packed with people and goods. Often they had music to fill the air and at evening there was a carnival air about the entire fjord with the twinkling lights on the buoys, the piers and the clusters of wooden chalets on shore. The purity of the air was as heady as the effect of sparkling champagne.

The pilotage authorities divided the intricate fjords into two sections, south and west; we were very familiar with the latter, entering at Lodingen and proceeding under the shelter of the Lofoten Islands, to Honningsvaag, passing Tromso en route. This diversion on the way to the White Sea fishing grounds cut out a long arduous run round the top of Norway and was well worth the pilot's fee. Either route, during the winter months, could be fraught with danger, especially when visibility was poor or nil. The pilots preferred the German trawlers because of the way their sidelights were positioned on the bows for narrow waterways such as the Rhine. A light kiss on those cruel rocks, and those monstrous teeth got an eternal grip, if the sea was angry close inshore, (as it never seemed to be anything else), the vessel would be pounded and ground out of existence, whatever the tonnage or bulk of the stricken vessel. An anchor was hung out of the hawse pipe on entering these waters, to drop instantly on the approach of fog or snow.

The pilots would take and post letters for us and if we were running regular trips they would deliver letters addressed to the ship. To re-enter the fjords after a gruelling, strenuous, storm-tossed period of fishing was second only to arriving home. Often we had a deck load of fish to put away in the comfort and shelter of the mountains. There were, no more than elsewhere, odd vessels going aground and when one trawler was sunk, *S.T. Aquamarine*, there was a temporary ban on using these waters; eventually, however, it was made obligatory to have two pilots on board. We went through one trip, in company with the *S.T. Keverne*, and after dropping our pilots at Honningsvaag we led the way in the dark hours out to sea. A few minutes later, there suddenly broke in on our radio, "Jim, are you there, I'm ashore". Sure enough when we turned we came across her still inside the rocky headland. After an hour of tugging and straining to pull her off, while the pilots firmly insisted that we would never do it, and that all vessels that grounded here were a total loss, we gave it a rest. Naturally, whenever any vessel went ashore, it was always the same tale from the locals, if the crew could be persuaded to leave it, there were good pickings to be had all round. Customarily, if a ship was abandoned even temporarily, the first person going aboard had a strong claim on it.

There was no lack of helpers to get a lot of the coal out of her and after this lightening up and greatly assisted by a rising tide, we managed to drag her off the hard ground. Leaking badly, though we got extra pumps on board, we succeeded in reaching Tromso and beached the vessel on a sandy beach, where she was made sea-worthy enough to reach home where she would need practically a new bottom. For the rest of the trip we estimated the salvage money due to us on our return, which, coupled with a good trip, would put us in clover. It was a bad trip for the other crew, but certainly not for us: that was fishing, 'the luck of the draw', "Yer takes a dip and Bobs yer Uncle", as the saying went. Our skipper was Lucky Jim, if he fell overboard he wouldn't get wet!

Of course there were some men who had gained a reputation, quite unwillingly, of being a veritable Jonah, through having been in some mishap or misfortune on some vessel or vessels. On any ship having a rough time, often one of the crew would be singled out, for the least reason, to bear the brunt of the men's resentment, though, more times than not, it was unfounded, just outright bullying.

This homecoming I decided that, having sufficient sea time in, I would sign off in order to attend the Hull Nautical School for Fishermen and have a shot at gaining a Mate's 'ticket'. To stay home for this reason, one had to save enough cash to tide one over for the few weeks attendance as no other financial support was available. We had to put ourselves out of work and were just not available to sail.

The school was a fair sized modern building consisting of two stages, the top one for boys intended for the Merchant Navy, the lower for fishermen whose ages ranged from nineteen to about forty, of whom there was a constant change of class of twenty or so, all under one instructor, who at that time (in the early 1930's;) was a very competent teacher, nothing at all like the proverbial schoolmaster. The school had a flat roof which was a replica of a ship's deck with bridge, masts and rigging. I could cheerfully have signed on that ship for quite a spell. Most of the men had left their elementary school as early as possible to eke out their family income and had to start again from scratch at the nautical school. To attend, one had to have the necessary sea time in, four years actually at sea to train for mate, a further year as mate to train for a skipper; time ashore in between was not counted. The time spent at school was quite a pleasant change from sea-going, a nine to four job, and dressed for the office, even down to the brief case for books and homework, but for all their indomitable courage no one ever dared to flaunt a furled umbrella.

There was an awful lot to be learned; at the beginning it seemed an impossible task. At times enlightenment came spontaneously, at others, it was sheer slogging. I well remember how perplexing it was that half multiplied by half, gave a lesser figure, and that a higher number could be subtracted from say one. Our teacher had a difficult, exasperating job, yet he managed to push so many through the Board of Trade examinations. Whenever he was absent through illness etc. a thirteen year old boy from upstairs would take over his duties, very capably too. There was one burly chap in his forties, a very experienced and trusted fellow, his firm had persuaded him to sit his ticket though he didn't 'stand a cat in hells chance' when it came down to 'brass tacks'. I doubt whether he had ever had any schooling whatever, like several of his age. The teacher's patience was sorely tested, but arithmetic to him was something foreign; yet we all envied his seamanship. The leeway in his learning could not be made good in the space of a few weeks. It did not come easy to us, the Cosines and Constants, Logs, Sines and Tangents, not forgetting a grounding in Astronomy and the use of complicated tables to work out sextant angles. Such sums and calculations took the full page of an exercise book to unravel. Most of us had never heard of maths or even trigonometry, worse luck, they just were not part of the elementary schools curriculum in our time. Neither he nor I qualified.

I must relate this story here (taking your indulgence for granted). It may have come down through the ages from Noah of the Ark but at least it's not even tinted 'blue'.

The inquisitor asked a bright young spark undergoing his B.O.T. oral exam,

"Let's suppose you are at anchor, off an unfriendly coast in a rising storm".

"Drop another anchor", sniggered he.

"But it got worse and worse".

"Drop another one" smirked he

Not getting the answer wanted, the harassed official came back with, "But by now there's an almighty gale". It failed to shake his confidence.

"Drop another"

"But where are you getting all those anchors from?"

"Same place as you're getting all that wind."

Whether he passed is not known. Those men who studied further and gained their extra Skippers Ticket were praiseworthy.

CHAPTER THIRTEEN

The following accounts are just simple jottings, in pencil, from an old note book.

1929 – 1930, September, October, November, December, January, sailed in the S.T. Thomas Hardy, skipper Harry Archer, average earnings £10000 per trip of 20 – 24 days. Catches of mixed fish from about 35 – 45 miles E. by N. of the North Cape, Iceland. Remarks: Gales frequent, worked ordinary otter trawl, cracks rare (damage to gear).

1930, sailed in Kingstons S.T. Chalcedony, skipper Ralph Cobby, March, April, May, Iceland, working Thorlack Roads, when weather decent catches of jumbo haddock and cod, Icelandic vessels with us salting. 1400 kits, fourteen days fishing, average £800.

June, July. Fished all round Iceland, very slack, poor trips (evidently not worthy of mention in the book).

August. Relief skipper, Iceland, tried close in, Red Sands Bay, plenty of small plaice, towing so shallow, top of trawl boards cutting water, had to clear out, policeman about (patrol boat).

September, October. Iceland. Grabbed fish wherever and whenever fine.

November. Iceland. At the whaleback (an unlit small rocky isle resembling a whales back out of water, about thirty miles from the mainland). Working French gear in deep water, lost lots of cod through towing too long. Got a quick trip in to be home in under fifteen days for £800.

Thomas Hardy - 1930

One could sail for Iceland, fish in the waters to the South'ard and return having not seen the mainland, when the fish was there to be had.

After a much needed spell ashore in 1930 I joined a fine newly built trawler with Iceland John, the skipper owner, an educated man who spoke good English until he swore, then it was 'blooty this' and 'blooty that'.

The ship was my best signing on so far, she was equipped with wireless and carried a Marconi operator; she also carried another new innovation, a prototype electrically operated depth sounder, which was a Godsend, while at the same time it destroyed any peace on board. When operated on the bridge, a hammer struck a plate atop the keel: This sent a shock wave to the sea bed which was echoed back and was measured and recorded by the machine on the bridge. This was a Fathometer: later types were much more sophisticated and quieter and the hammer method was scrapped. The skipper also improved the crew's quarters, a mess room on the deck aft side of and adjoining the galley. Also there was a roomy square shaped hole set right in the bows. The net store was relegated to that position. It solved another problem, one I never understood why it was not altered for years; the fo'scle stove funnel jutted about six feet above the Whaleback, so that the first sea the vessel went head first into, the funnel was swept away and water teemed down onto the hot coals, causing extreme discomfort for days or weeks.

Our mate was a Norwegian Viking, Martin Dalgreevs, the bosun Russian Alex, whose hands were massive (he) could span the largest dinner plates and raise them up; he never slept or to be more precise he never closed his eyes). Norwegian Walter was a good cook; he would produce excellent cream cakes from tinned milk and bottles of pop by inserting a knob of yeast before corking. I helped him put six large joints of meat in brine and saltpetre, which when the other joints that were buried in ice had been consumed, proved to be delicious. Two deckhands were Danes – Hans Larsen and Petersen.

The building of the vessel had put the skipper £25,000 in the red but, by the end of the first year, the whole cost had been earned and paid over, a remarkable accomplishment.

Other useful extras were a couple of hip baths, which were small, but most men could squeeze into them, and two hand basins to replace buckets. Fresh water was a very big problem for all shipping but more so for trawlers, therefore baths were taboo. Such improvements in the crew's comforts annoyed other firms who would be expected to follow suit and the skipper had considerable opposition to overcome. Never-the-less he succeeded and went on to own further ships, which on the outbreak of war, were taken over by the 'powers that be', and John was sent to the Isle of Man. Later he held the position of Icelandic Consul in Hull.

Two of the crew had left the ship to have Christmas at home. I was quick to take one place being always of the opinion that Christmas could be enjoyed anywhere and anytime. I was unmarried and intended to remain so; marriage was not an ideal state for us, constantly at sea and at risk. I had been orphaned early and did not wish any offspring of mine to be so unfortunate. During the war I spent two Christmases thousands of miles from home in hostile waters, in the tropics; they are, however, best forgotten.

When we signed on the *S.T. Kopanes*, named after the skipper's birthplace, he assured us that we would be having Christmas dinner alongside the pier at Tromso, nothing could be more ideal. He was a true gentleman! The ship had done two trips to Bear Island, bringing in £1900 and £1700, quite good totals at that time. Now it was the White Sea and we sailed on December 19th 1930 and arrived at Tromso to berth amidst several German trawlers who were always good company and extremely free with the cases of cognac they were never without. The picturesque surroundings, from the snow capped mountains, down through the Swiss-like chalets to the still blue waters of the tiny harbour with the quaint shaped boats, could not be surpassed we thought, but when evening came upon us we were spellbound. It was a fairyland of countless flickering lights, like as if the star studded heavens had come down to embrace us. Many Christmas trees twinkled merrily outside the chalets. We trudged happily through the crisp snow and couldn't resist trying out the cycles on skis, favoured by the locals.

One fisherman invited me to his chalet; in the porch were a few pairs of overshoes, (no one could enter a house in their outdoor footwear). Inside was a stove in the centre with a long funnel going up through the roof. The walls were covered in many thicknesses of newspapers and magazines with the pictures showing to their advantage, all very warm and cosy, and colourful. There was quite a colony of Laplanders wintering here mostly with their quaint tents, and as the mountains in this region once abounded with silver fox, hunting was an added attraction. Popular purchases here were furs, dolls and slippers of catfish skin trimmed with fur with the toes curled up like the prows of their boats. There were also slippers were made from sealskin.

One had to be careful when buying furs, the Norwegians round about there knew little of curing them beyond wind drying and salting them, but the Laplanders knew much less and left out the salting. A bonny Lapland doll dressed in furs began to smell after a few days, and on opening its fur coat there was blood on the inside. Usually a silver fox fur was taken to a furrier on arrival home and cured properly making a much prized stole. On complaining of one fur shedding its hairs after curing, I was told that the animal had been dead some time before skinning. The most common fur was the sealskin; the Laplanders had round bottomed boats so that when seal hunting and drifting ice closed on them they were lifted bodily clear of the water and could carry the boat to open water again.

On the radio we now had reports from vessels on various grounds, and after weighing up the pro's and con's we left the fjords and headed northerly for that bleak island that rose out of the sea like a crouching bear:

> Fishing in complete darkness all the twenty- four hours, a good way to the Westward of the Isle. All cod and sprags, nets torn only when loaded with fish, weather fine, not much frost, using ordinary gear. Landed on twentieth day 2000 ten stone kits, made £1890, also eighty-nine forty gallon wooden casks of cod livers.

> January, 1931, Iceland. On arrival ran down East about, passed vessels getting good living at the Whaleback, too many for it to last long. Got 1,200 kit good fish among puddings (sponges) about twenty to thirty miles North West of North Cape. When blowing fished close to Adlivick and Isa Fjord with French gear (cables), made short tows. Twenty-one days away, landed 1,200 kit made £1,300, on February 2nd, Monday. Some weather damage needed repairs.

> February 11th Iceland. Ran down East about, got trip from North Cape in 110 to 120 fath, just outside puddings, French gear, got along alright. Landed 1,500 kits of rough stuff, made £1,500.

> February 27th, Iceland. Ran down West about, shot abreast of Northerly slope of Snowy, an ever white topped mountain, using French gear five to six miles off, had two hauls, split from end to end. Steams to abreast of southerly slope, some distance off, shot ordinary gear, six foot legs, eleven, sometimes twelve lengths of

warp out from each drum, (25 faths. to a length), in general trawlers worked a warp length of around twice the depth, more in deep water. Two good bags of fish for half-an-hour, one third jumbo haddocks, the rest cod which stiffened immediately on release from the net, it was freezing hard. When 500 kit on deck, dodged in under shelter of the land, blowing. Wind veered south westerly to gale force, no frost now, for forty-eight hours uncomfortable, riding to a far flung anchor under Sandvig, when wind east, shot fourteen miles N.E., thirty baskets of round fish, four of flats, lemon soles, plaice, turbot and halibut, in fifty-two fathoms, grit and shell bottom. Wind veered, back to Snowy Joker, Forty-eight hours, more than 2,200 kit aboard. Landed Monday 16*th*, £1010, markets shocking, over supplied.*

Our electric sounder was proving its use and value, giving us the true depth in a matter of seconds, though we still kept at the ready the hand lead line of fourteen pounds weight and the twenty-eight pounder for deeper water. This, when cast, plunged down rapidly at first for perhaps fifty fathoms then, affected by the pressure well down, would slow and slow until we could scarcely tell whether it had reached the bottom or not: not too reliable in deep water. Before shooting the trawl a sounding used to be taken, but after lowering the trawl at full speed for about ten minutes, we were not sure what depth we were in; however, if the leads were primed with lard or dripping they did collect a bit of the sea bed for our information, which the machine could not provide. It could however, differentiate between a solid or soft sea bed by the strength of the return signal. We were now able to tow round the most profitable part of a bank, (the sloping edges) and maintain our depth, even to the extent of losing the bottom and quickly regaining it.

CHAPTER FOURTEEN

Now that trawlers were being built larger, they were able to have heavier and more powerful winches, and to carry more wire warp on the drums, enabling vessels to fish deeper and deeper. This, however, brought its own problems. The whole exercise was to keep the bottom of the trawl, mainly the footrope, on the sea bed, and the top part, the head rope, raised about six to ten feet above it, forming a huge mouth. On fine ground, using cables or ticklers ahead of the net, flat fish were stirred up out of their cosy beds in the sand, into the advancing net, but on rough ground they could snarl the gear into the most extraordinary cock-ups that were difficult to disentangle in bad weather, and these were to be avoided.

We sought fish on its habitat, not the chancy shoals on the move. Bottom and surface fishing were the types that brought concrete results. When mid-water trawling was embarked upon, it was never a success. Strong glass balls laced into net were good floats for the headline in ordinary depths and had stood us in good stead over the years, but in deep water they imploded. Metal floats of various kinds were substituted, the early types came up crushed like old tin cans, but eventually by trial and error, sets were made to withstand the pressure at over two hundred and fifty fathoms. Below that depth, the trawl was unreliable and the pressure was too much for the fish themselves.

There were changes in the gear too: for many years, outside of the North Sea, thick heavy wooden bobbins of up to fourteen inches in diameter were used in the footrope to lift and protect the main body of the net. Up to six sets of these bobbins could be worn out each trip; they covered so many miles of ground. Eventually came a shortage of suitable trees to produce such large bobbins.

Rubber tyred bobbins were tried which came up like burst car wheels, and concrete ones disintegrated. The most successful substitutes were those constructed of large iron balls, but even these suffered heavy wear and tear. Oblong tank shaped constructions were tried out with the patentee's idea that on hitting an object or obstruction they would topple over it; this they sometimes did dragging the net down under them with dire results.

The biggest change on our boats was from ordinary gear to French gear while an equivalent change was taking place in the smaller trawlers, which were adopting the very successful seine-net from Denmark, which was suitable for rough grounds or deep water.

The actual Granton trawl remained substantially unchanged, over many years, except in its size. A handy innovation about this time was a derrick on the foremast, though we tended to overdo its use, resulting in accidents and consequent injury. Ships were being built larger with boat decks added, and though more superstructures meant more space it also had many drawbacks. In icy conditions it provided more foothold for the ice to build on, in some cases with fatal results; it meant more tonnage to propel through the water, bigger engines, and more H.P., with little increase in speed and more wind resistance; indeed a high superstructure acted in the same way as a large sheet of canvas and when the vessel laid over she was all the more reluctant to get upright again. Metal hatch covers were replacing wooden ones cutting out tarpaulins, battens and wedges.

Patented ideas sprang up all the time. One fellow took out a patent for metal bunker lids, copied from the screw inside the tops of lemonade bottles, and very successful it was too.

To return to that dog-eared old note book, with scribbled jottings that for some strange reason has managed not to stray and which has now proved to be a big help to me in delving into the past:

Left dock March 18th, 1931, Iceland. Getting fifty to sixty baskets at the Whaleback. Steamed on, passed Lord Fisher towing, never spoke, fishermen are like farmers, when asked "How's business", it was always bad. Steamed four and a half miles off Rod-a-Ruk N.W. by W.½.W. Dahn buoy down in sixty fathoms, shot ordinary gear, ten baskets of plaice, daylight, twenty in the dark. Steamed a hundred miles to Scraggy Corner, Dahn buoy down in sixty fathom, E.S.E. of corner, flats, thirty of haddocks, a few split nets. Landed 280 kits of flats, 350 of haddock, 300 of cod. Easter Monday, April 6th, markets pretty fair, £1890.

Left dock April 8th, 1931, N.E. by N.¾.N. from Spurn Lightship, bound White Sea, fine run to Fjords, plenty of timber boats awaiting ice free reports from Archangel. On leaving at Honninsvaag, steamed to Sem Island, breasted light, single sharp flash, shot nine miles off, forty baskets several flats, tried thirty miles E. by S. shot along edge of polar ice barrier, wind E. cannot get right off where reports of good fishing came from. Wind changed to S.W. ice slowly moves northerly we trawl along following it. Bouy down in seventy odd fathom, twenty-two baskets of flats. After forty-eight hours lifted buoy, towed off along edge of ice, finally reaching fifty odd miles east of island, outside of coral, split nets if we got on coral. Ten days fishing, 4,800 stones of plaice, 1,500 stones mostly haddock. Surrounded with drifting ice, time to beat a hasty retreat southerly to Tanner fjord. Buoy down four miles S.W. of corner, ducks and plaice inside of buoy, double bags of cod and sprags outside. Landed May 4th, Monday. 450 kits of plaice, 150 haddocks, 300 kits of rough stuff. Markets fair.

This was a fisherman's paradise. In twenty hours with two hundred and fifty kit on deck and little room below for it, we had to head for Honningsvaag in a freshening wind and snow showers.

By now a depression was sweeping the whole of the U.K., and ships were being laid up in every port. There just wasn't the money about, good quality fish remained unsold and went to the fertilizer factory, and everybody was cutting costs. Within weeks, half the fishing fleet was idle and the merchant fleets fared even worse.

Big catch

When a ship landed and the crew visited the office to collect monies due there were many ex shipmates on hard times, who were glad of the odd note slipped into their pocket. This was a custom that often was repaid with interest, being much appreciated by those in need.

Left dock May 9th, bound White Sea, wireless reports good fishing cod and haddock at Sulter Fjord, passed through them (why catch cod when it failed to sell back home) *on to Sem Island, shot close in, then steamed fifty days, 220 kit, steamed to Sylti fjord, all cod, shot off Verone Rocks, haddock and cod, steamed to Vardoe shot off Perse Fjord, two bags of fish for half hours tow, two thirds haddock. Norwegian boats came alongside and crew came aboard to help us get fish below, their help much appreciated, gave them all fish less than two feet long, they filled their boats and were happy. Fine ground, using French gear, 1000 kit of which 950 were haddock in three days fishing, then the fish shifted elsewhere. Steam for Tanner Fjord, double bags, one third ducks, twenty-four hours fishing and the fish was gone, steamed for Honninsvaag. Landed Wed. June 3rd, 220 kit of plaice, 950 of haddock, 300 of rough stuff, markets no good for cod, made £1560.* Today the rough stuff alone would fetch more than that.

Norwegian Walter, our cook, had a trick, much hated by the crew, of lowering overboard a wooden box lid with a fish nailed in the centre. Gannets with their marvellous sight would spot this from over two hundred feet above and dive down with incredible speed. There would be an awful bang and the cook would retrieve it, its beak having been pushed through its head and out the back. He would then cook and partake of it with relish. Gannets were not liked by most fishermen as they were the scavengers of the deep and were so greedy that they would fly around with half a cod protruding from their beaks, waiting for the inner half to digest, but we still let him see our disgust, though it pleased him to rile us. Even Russian Alex eventually could not stomach it any longer and one day went for him with a knife. If the cool, calm, authoritative voice of the skipper had not intervened, the cook would have met the same fate as those unfortunate gannets.

No ship was ever looked after better; in the fjords the skipper had bought a good supply of Stockholm tar, and we coated the decks, rigging, wires and ourselves in the process. It is wonderful stuff to work with, very preserving and smells nice too.

During the trip I had been reading of 'Lawrence of Arabia', and his passion for speeding along country roads on his Brough Superior motorbike. My hobby was tinkering with mechanical things and this had fired my imagination. My mind was made up, and though loath to leave this, my best ship so far, I signed off against the skipper's advice. I had to answer the call to two wheels. Besides, I wanted a boatswain's job and Russian Alex was there for good. I had the money, the opportunity and it was the best time of year.

The showroom manager was not very co-operative when I put down my £150 and asked for a Brough Superior. He smiled and asked, "Do you know that is the Rolls Royce of bikes, one just doesn't pass one over the counter like that, it could take months, besides it's not for a beginner, I'll show you what you want" and he extolled the virtues, in turn, of a Sun, a Dot, a Frances Barnet and an Excelsior. Even I could tell him they were two-strokes and I wanted a super-bike. "I'll show you some at half the price of a Brough Superior." Indeed, there was a baffling array. Ariel, Calthorpe, B.S.A., Indian, Norton, Matchless, Sunbeam, Douglas, Panther, Rudge, Scott, Vincent and Velocette. I decided on an all black, gold-lettered A.J.S., big port, 350 cc, and collected it the next day. I got it home with the help of an instruction book and a long hard trek, but my heart was light. It was mine, every nut and bolt, I had earned it and I was prouder than a peacock was of its tail; when I made my triumphal entry into my road, people came out to admire it, "He's certainly on the up and up, and still only a deckhand at that". "There'll be no holding him now" and "A good lass would have done him more good". They were soon to hate the very sight and sound of it, all hours of the night and day. Well one cannot please everyone and some may have been right, who knows.

There were a few comely wenches, curiously, just passing my humble abode whenever I emerged. Also there was a Customs Preventative Officer a few doors away, who was evidently, because of his job I supposed, rather a persevering type. He had thirteen daughters before giving up hopes of a son: He would extol their many virtues and proclaim them as such a delectable choice. They all did eventually marry but their marriages must have exhausted his savings if any, and what a life he must have led. I could not hide my comings and goings and when returning with a pronounced limp heads would wag, even coming home in the late hours of the early morning would not go unnoticed nor unremarked upon. Sometimes I impishly created grounds for gossip to enliven someone's drab life. I soon loved to speed through the deserted town in the early hours and on out into the inky black of the countryside, headlights probing the blackness and turning night into day, finally to halt at the cliff edge and gaze at the sea shimmering in the moonlight.

I joined a local club and took part in trials, grass track, and road races and was soon one of a gang but preferred being on my own.

From Hull it was a days outing to Knaresborough, Blackpool, the whole of the Lake District and many other places. I also went on to join the local flying club which I loved but with my time ashore in a year my activities were limited.

One evening we left the Gipsyville Tavern after a bet with the landlord that we would be drinking in the Spreadeagle at Withernsea, twenty-five miles distant, in under half an hour, not knowing how long it would take to get the eight miles through the town before reaching a clear road. Our bet was won when the Spreadeagle's landlord 'phoned through to say we were in his bar inside the stated time. It was not until the next year that we invaded the Isle of Man.

One friend, a T.T. rider, complained of my cornering and took me out to improve it. He mounted the pillion as we neared a notorious S bend and said "Take this at speed; whatever happens do not touch the brakes, don't panic, if you're not going to make it I'll get you round". The road was strewn with gravel. I slid round the first bend but entering the second I knew I wasn't going to make it, panicked and lightly touched the brake: instantly we were a goner. He came towards me, one side of his face like raw meat dotted with pebbles. "You touched the brake". Thoroughly ashamed I nodded. "Ha! I knew it", he said and smiled. We carried on to the hospital where they had a tedious job with his pebble-dashed face, and rode home still pals, my admission having vindicated his honour.

> *June 10th, 1931. Left dock in S.T. Cassie, skipper Frank Furnley, nearing Scotland, learnt we were sitting on a time bomb, the coal in the bottom of the bunkers was smouldering, threatening to break out and engulf the ship. Radio orders were to proceed to Aberdeen, not to enter harbour but go alongside a pier where the fire brigade took over. Most of the coal had to be removed before the seat of the fire was got at. The cause was spontaneous combustion.*

On arrival at Iceland, we ran up the east side and shot at Scraggy Bank. Within hours we received a radio order from head office in

Hull, "Proceed to square H.2." which proved to be a well off Isa Fjord, over a hundred miles away round the northern tip of Iceland. There was an exceptionally large mass of floating summer ice to get through, but it was daylight all the twenty-four hours and when we arrived there at the stated position, there was not a smoke in sight. We found a little of good prime fish off Adlivick, but were soon off back to the East'ard, a radio report was on its way via Cullercoats to that effect. West of Grimsey Isle we found forty to a hundred baskets of good sprags and were set for a decent catch. Greatly to the skipper's disgust, a reply came from the owners, "Go back, carry out orders". We carried on fishing until it was estimated we had sufficient on board to clear our expenses, then the skipper apologised to us and headed for home. We fully agreed with him and his course of action, though we all knew the consequences to expect. He was definitely finished and so it proved. As for us, it was a fore-gone conclusion; we were all going to sign off knowing it would be difficult to re-ship again. A firm could blacklist anyone on all the other firms' books, but we were determined to support our skipper. We landed July 1st, 750 ten stone kits, £260, barely clearing expenses; all we got was our meagre wages, less cost of sea gear, tobacco etc. A trip best forgotten, because of a modern aid, or more correctly, the misuse of it.

While undergoing the long and duly expected compulsory spell walking the pebbles, a well known skipper, Jimmy Myers saw me and insisted on me signing on his ship the Cape Finisterre, despite my still being on the black list. Over November and December we got two satisfactory trips from Bear Isle, £1300, and a £1500, then in January sailed for Iceland. We found plenty of cod on Dyra Fjord bank and prime fish off Patrik's fjord, Landing 1200 ten stone kits, we made £1120.

There followed three more trips from Iceland, along the south coast, the Whale-back, the Hoof and the Horns, fairly comfortable trips as regards the weather.

> *Early April 1932, Iceland, Cape Matapan, Jack Barnes skipper, got trip west of the westernmost island of the Vestmannaeyjar*

Isles. Landed 1600 ten stone kits, made £450, left.

May 3rd, left dock Cape Guardifui (Neils Oram), Iceland. Get haddock off Thulok and cod west of the Horns. Landed 1,300 kit made £1200.

Third trip, left dock May 20th, ran down west about, reports of ice on east side. Got N.N.E. of North Cape, had fifty baskets haddock, flats and cats over a yard long and very fierce. Towed southerly away from approaching ice. Steamed easterly all hands chopping ice from ship, kept going to the Horns on the south coast. Good catches of cod. Landed Wed. June 8th, £450 for 1620 ten stone kit.

The depression was still taking its toll.

Left dock June 10th, ran down east-about, shot E. of Cape, steamed N.N.W. of Cape, close up to ice barrier, got thirty baskets of sprags, same of Coal-fish, few flats. Shot West of Cape, about the same, shot close in to Rita Ruk, steamed to Grim's isle, little better, steamed to Langanes, still troubled with drifting ice growlers. Sixty to a hundred baskets of cod and sprags. Steamed to Gletinganes and towed down across Seydis Fjord, eleven lengths of warp out, seventy baskets of cod and sprags. Steamed to the Horns, then Stokesnes and Duck Island, haddock, flats and codling, on to Whaleback. Landed 1,200 kit, made £470.

CHAPTER FIFTEEN

Left dock Thurs. July 14th. Went to Aberdeen, boiler tube trouble.

Trawlers had one of two types of boiler. The early ones were water chamber boilers: a round drum of water (the fire box hot flues pass through tubes) heating the water which is about two thirds of the way up the drum. The tubes are at their hottest above the level of the water, which gives off steam, filling the top part of the chamber. Our later type was a water tubed boiler; the water ran through the tubes, turning to steam on its path through the firebox, eventually giving off steam and in later types superheated steam. Both types gave little trouble and when they did, tubes could be individually blocked off, but to do any boiler repairs meant reducing the pressure and the heat and could be very awkward in certain circumstances, leaving the ship at the mercy of the elements.

> *Repairs done, on to Iceland, shot close in to Isa Fjord, haddock, Dahn down three miles off corner. After three days went to Dyra Fjord bank, seventy kit a day, tried off Blacknes, back to the bank. Bad weather, steamed to Portland, plenty of coalies. Landed 900 kit, made £2820. Wed. Aug. 3rd.*

Iceland had purchased from the UK a modern fleet of trawlers, but instead of fishing they were finding it more profitable to load up from their numerous small craft and ferry the fish to Hull, often ruining the markets for our fish. German trawlers were also dumping surplus catches here.

The crews of ships with radios could now, about thirty six hours before being due to dock, send a radio telegram of their E.T.A to their relatives who could meet the ship at the quay and have a ride through the docks. This was popular especially with the children, who were all over the ship, but occasionally it had some sad results, bringing to mind the phrase "There's many a slip twixt cup and lip".

One unfortunate crew of the Lady Jeanette, which steamed up the river on a freezing cold wintry night and was unable to approach the quay until the tide was high enough, (as was the usual practice), dropped its anchor near midstream. Within minutes a terrible tragedy occurred. In full view of waiting relatives and sweethearts, the vessel's anchor dragged, the stern touched a sandbank causing the vessel to capsize. The screams of those trapped on board and those in the fast flowing icy water swept miles up river could be heard on shore. All hands were drowned and only the top of the vessel's masts marked its watery grave. The River Humber can be treacherous with its strong tides and sand banks.

On another occasion, we left Bear Island in company with the Admiral Collingwood, for the same market, though we expected her to show us a clean pair of heels as she was a fine vessel, new and on her maiden voyage. The two skippers were in regular contact with each other and when it was clear, we could sight her getting well ahead; in fact our skipper asked him, when he arrived, to let the folks know that we were not far behind and that he might have given us a tow. After logging 388 miles on run to Skemvaer (a treacherous landmark because of the rocky reefs running well out to sea)', the turning point for the run across the North Sea to the Humber. It being a rough night and keeping well off, we failed to pick the flash-light up and, on the logged mileage done, altered course for home. To our great concern there was no radio call from our friend that morning, or during the day. Radios were not too reliable we knew, but when we still failed to make contact we were full of foreboding and reported the matter by radio as the weather was bad.

On arrival at the dock head, several people inquired of us about the non-arrival of the expected vessel. There was little we could truthfully say, except hope for the best, but she never did arrive: another mystery of the sea. If, as is most probable, she grounded at Svin, she would have been annihilated in minutes, the wreckage completely obliterated.

That August I left ship; whenever we did this we forfeited our right to draw the dole, but if we were sacked it was different, thus, on the last day at sea, the mate sometimes received an unprovoked, unasked for, thump on the nose, which deservedly merited the boot. If the bosun was the smaller of the two, he would be singled out for the assault.

When ashore, there were several different brews of local beer of which to partake. One in particular resulted in a very melancholy state of mind, with a desperate longing to sob ones heart out on the nearest shoulder, while another brew turned the meekest person into a veritable Jack Johnson, causing trouble all round. To imbibe a mixture of both was fatal, ones mind was in an awful turmoil as you can imagine. I well remember one young fellow who had evidently been on the second mentioned brew, sparring round a big chap in the city centre. He paused and divested himself of his coat, hat, scarf and very smart jacket, throwing them to the crowd that were gathering, and proceeded to throw punches at his selected opponent. I came along, and seeing my harmless friend had picked on someone twice his size, I shouted the first word that came into my head, in those days, a powerful one, "POLICE". Immediately the crowd melted away and to my unfortunate friend's consternation, his possessions and valuables had melted away with them leaving him in his rolled up shirt sleeves, his muscles like sparrows' knees.

One chap was never without a pint. He had sustained an injury at sea and would approach a group at a table in a pub or club and suggest bets on who could span with the hand the furthest. When they had finished putting their marks on the table he would plonk his thumb down and say "My little finger's off Iceland, beat that!" Of course we all paid out; no matter how often we were caught. Another chap would stick a penknife in his leg, not everyone knew it was an artificial one! There were a good number of men who had suffered injury at sea, from frostbite or the result of accidents and several were specially employed in making baskets etc. in a place on the dock provided for them.

> *Left dock in Cape Kanin, skipper Albert Harmer, bound Iceland, Aug. 18th 1932. Had serious engine trouble after leaving the Pentland Firth well astern.*

One cylinder head blew off which put us in a very awkward situation, wallowing in a rough sea with no radio. We gradually drifted off the beaten track and could expect no help. Under emergency temporary repairs we managed to reach Tershavn in the Faroe Islands: to drill out sheared off cylinder head bolts and fit new ones was a simple job for a workshop, but even so, the breakdown almost caused the loss of the ship with all hands. Continuing our voyage north we shot our gear at Snowy.

> *Twenty miles north then E.N.E, best twenty-five baskets. Steamed to seventeen miles N.N.E. of Stalberg corner in forty fathom, strong winds, towed upwards to close off Isa Fjord to get under the lee of the mountain. Getting thirty baskets, half of which were haddock, a few nice halibut, and the odd 'Genii' of up to fifty stones in weight.*

Genii were giant halibut that had to be handled with a winch and tackle individually and gently lowered down the fish room. They realized good money back home. The Icelandic fisheries patrol boat insisted we pick up our dahn and clear off.

> *Steamed to three miles N.W. of Dyra Fjord, towed out a mile, thirty-five baskets, few flats, steamed further off, same results, steamed to Breidi Fjord, finished trip off there. Landed 700 kit (200 haddock) Thurs. Sept. 8th. Made £1060.*

On the next trip two refrigeration engineers were coming with us, and one fish room was to be used for tests with cooling apparatus. There were hopes of using much less ice yet still keeping the earliest caught fish in better condition than it generally was. To have educated men on board, unconnected with fishing, living a different life, was most welcome. During the summer months a trawler was affected by any heat, which caused the ice that the fish was buried in to melt leaving the fish unprotected. On a sunny day a cold water hose kept running on the foredeck, once the hatches were battened down at the end of fishing they were not opened until the fish was to be landed. Skippers used to avoid anchoring too long in the warmer water of the river, by staying in the estuary until the tide was right to go up and dock, and often the water in the dock was warm. In the winter months there was no need for further cooling, the people in the 1930's did not want frozen fish, and neither did the trade. This testing period was not to freeze but only to prevent the ice melting. The two passengers proved very good company, particularly during the long night watches, but were kept busy when fishing commenced.

> *Sailed Fri. Sept. 9th, Iceland. Shot S.S.W. of Salberg corner, good fishing but nets split, towed of S.W. lost fish. Shot three miles of Dyra Fjord, peer steamed off to forty fathom. Thirty baskets first haul, during the second tow the vessel came fast making no headway through the water.*

It was difficult to get the trawl up, there was a great weight in the nets, which to our surprise were sluthers (jelly-fish): they were a nuisance, and soon had us hopping mad with their stinging tentacles. A splash from them would burn the face.

> *Steamed to inner ground in Breidi Fjord, flats and codling, dhan down. Shifted at dark to middle ground, 150 kit of sprags and few flats for one night. Landed 800 kit (80 of haddock, 130 of flats) made £890 on Friday Sept. 30th. Trouble with unloading the refrigerated fish room, the ice and fish took some separating,*

The fish were mainly frozen and the unloaders demanded extra money. The merchants were also reluctant to buy this fish and the idea was scrapped as a failure until several years later when specially built freezer trawlers, designed to stay on the fishing grounds longer, came into general use. Whilst in dock we were equipped with a radio telephone, mainly for use between vessels.

> *Sailed Sat. Oct. 1st, Iceland. Shot S.S.W. of Stalberg Corner but soon had to shelter from a near gale in Breidi Fjord. Twenty-four hours later fished on inner and middle grounds, for three days unable to get far off the land. Steamed to Stalberg Corner, fished in forty fathom, opening and shutting Patricks Fjord. Bad weather, steamed to Portland, the Whaleback and carried on to Kidney Bank. Got 105 kit of shelved cod, 100 of coalies, 50 of soldiers for forty-eight hours work, also 120 of flats and 50 of ducks. Landed 720 kit on Monday Oct. 24th, made £933.*

> *Sailed again the next day, Oct. 25th, Iceland. One day was sufficient for refuelling, repairs, taking on over 200 tons of ice, stocking of provisions and required replacement of fishing gear and the refilling of water tanks etc. Trawled off Stalberg Corner towards Patricks Fjord, twenty baskets and five of flats. Steamed to Dyra Fjord, same amount of fish. After thirty-six hours steamed to Isa Fjord, on to Rita Ruk, bad weather, dodged back to Dyra Fjord, spent three days at anchor. Found forty baskets off Stalberg Corner, blowing hard, three days in Patricks Fjord, at anchor.*

At Patricks Fjord a boat came alongside and an Icelander wanted to sell a couple of puppy dogs, Iceland Poms, bonny little bundles of fur. "Man dogs" he said, "Rattle when shaken", and went through the motions. Unwisely, one fellow could not resist the urge to have one, and thus we had a newcomer on board. After another twenty-four hours fishing in bad conditions, with no decent weather forecasts, we headed for home. We landed 426 kit, 81 of flats and made £640 on Sat. Nov. 19th. When the customs men came aboard on arrival they lifted the trapdoor to the chain locker down the forecastle. One shone his torch down and, as two eyes glared back at him, called to his mate "Have a look at this rat down here"... His mate said, "That's no rat, it's a dog". The fellow it belonged to had to declare it and it had to go into quarantine for six months, but when he got it back it was admired by many.

CHAPTER SIXTEEN

Seldom did we go ashore at Iceland, the terrain was rocky with snow drifts. At dark it was positively dangerous to wander about and the people were very reserved, but when in the fjords, if we wished, they would sometimes get a village hop going to accordion music. They lived a Spartan life, mainly fishing for their staple diet, and they cultivated small plots of ground on the sheltered slopes of the mountain sides, with some success; they also had a little livestock. The schools and hospitals were mainly run by the Danes. Bottles of questionable wine could be found in a small hotel; one kind tasted like methylated spirit and had the same noxious effects. They did not want our money and preferred to barter, though they had very little to offer. When their vessels landed at Hull, they bought up everything they could afford, even cycles to take home.

Iceland belonged to Denmark until it gained independence; its area is about 42,000 square miles and the coastline presents a continuous succession of deep fjords and bays, penetrating far inland except along the south coast. It is an ice covered plateau, built up of volcanic rocks in the centre, uninhabitable, and is crowned with perpetual snow and ice. Across the island the volcanic agency is still active and terrible eruptions have repeatedly occurred within the last four centuries and beyond. The best known are Hekla, Katla and Askja but one of the greatest was that of recent years when a mountain of fire and brimstone erupted violently out of the sea in the area of Vestmannaeyjar Isles, smothering the islands with fire and molten lava. A whole new island, Surtsey, emerged from the sea. Any trawler fishing anywhere near that area must have thought that the end of the world had come.

A large proportion of Iceland is covered by lava and the hot springs or geysers scattered throughout the island are other specimens of volcanic agency. These are mainly found in the S.W. where one of the main geysers throws up at intervals, jets of water, stones and mud to a height varying from 100 to 200 feet. Mount Hekla (1491 metres high) is a magnificent scene of great volcanic natural beauty. Trees were almost non-existent except for a few small stunted birch.

Vegetation was scarce and the inhabitants were dependent on grasses for their live-stock. The polar bear was an occasional visitor, no doubt when the polar ice barrier reaches the mainland, but reindeer were introduced around 1770. Many Scandinavian migrants settled there from about 1860 onwards.

Late in the 1920's we were told that there were no prisons there as we knew them, wrongdoers were given work to do and the worst of them were sent to toil in sulphur and salt mines. Polar bear skins and fur could be obtained but they were rare, so magnificent they were.

Along the south coast at Ingolfs Hofde, Skeidara Sands and Bruna Sands, at the scene of several shipwrecks, there were well constructed shelters for shipwrecked mariners to make for, which were equipped with provisions, heating, lighting and the means of signalling to the nearest farms. Nearby were directions and sign posts in several languages, even portable boats.

Ships sometimes went ashore on this coast, seeking a landfall when nearing Iceland and drawn ashore by false compass readings due to local magnetic influence. One Hull trawler on only its second trip when new, the Kingston Jasper, was lost along this coast. The north-west coast was also a dangerous place. A Hull trawler, *Macbeth*, grounded there and surveyors gave it up as a bad job. A local farmer on the high rocks above bought it for £10 and some months later it landed a catch of fish at Hull. For most vessels that went ashore, even before radio, their fate or net was generally known, but of those that were overwhelmed under tons of ice or water, theirs was a mystery, an unexplained disappearance. The *St. Louis* was one of these. She was last seen or heard of shortly after leaving the Humber and heading for off Norway in a strong following wind and sea.

Over the years several fishermen were lost overboard, whilst fishing or on passage. Some would not be missed until hours had elapsed. In one trawler at anchor in a fjord a very young member of the crew, in high spirits, dived overboard for a swim. The water was deceptively cold and he was not seen again. The wearing of rings on the fingers, or buttons on clothes were frowned upon, men were caught in the nets and drawn overboard because of this. Mittens or gloves were never worn when working above the deck, it was safest to trust one's own two hands no matter how numb or cold they were.

> *Sailed Nov. 21st bound Bear Island. Ran down to the deep waters S.W. of the island found fish in 190 fath., got some large puddings (sponges) and soldiers (red fish with spikes) amongst cod, towing one hour, eighteen lengths of warp out 450 fath off each drum. Also fish in 200 fath. Island bears N. by W. Landed 1,700 kit, made £750.*

I signed off to have Christmas ashore and was now sailing regularly as bosun, which meant having a berth in the cabin, one of the best parts of any ship with its polished wood panels, gleaming brass and nice stove. There was of course being close to the propeller to get used to, especially the bronze ones now in use, which set up a high pitched whistle, but it was much preferred to the ups and downs of the forecastle.

Christmas amongst the fishing community was full of festivity, but due to the large number of men at sea, there was always a strong religious influence in the background. Annually, at this time, there were the big social occasions, such as the Skippers and Mates Ball and the Bobbers Ball, where they left their usual footwear, clogs, at home. Generally the City Hall was taken over for these events and very successfully too.

The most noticeable community characteristics that stood out along the old Hessle Road (now spelled Hessel Road), was the sharing of friendship and hospitality in those houses huddled together in the closely knit streets. There were so many lonely mothers, widows and fatherless children to share everything with, happiness most of all, if only for a little while. Some firms on the dock held their separate functions giving us a chance to hob-nob with our bosses, perhaps they were human at times and didn't begrudge our time ashore.

Midnight mass at St. Wilfreds was a must, whatever party had to be left, and no matter what state we had got into. Taxis lined up outside after getting us there on time. One priest in his sermon, during this particular mass, always spoke of the huge congregation on that night, and truthfully told us, that for many, it was the one time in the year we ever came to church, hence we had not entirely deserted his flock, that there was still hope, however small, for us. A forthright, 'give it to 'em' man of the cloth, was to be respected even allowing for his Irish descent. Oh how we would sing that glorious hymn, "For those in peril on the sea," our hearts were reaching out to those hearts at sea, we meant and hung on every word.

We only enjoyed a Christmas like this every so many years; we therefore appreciated it, not surprisingly, in a big way. Just to visit the town and mingle in the happy crowds, see the brilliantly lit shops, and streets that for a time blotted out the terrible vastness and loneliness of the ocean. Yet, despite it all, it didn't seem real, sometimes we felt like fish out of water, and extraordinary, unbelieving though it seemed, relaxation came when we were once more 'rocking in the cradle of the deep', after the interruption, which after all, was what Christmas represented, was over. Of course, whilst home, one had to keep away from the vicinity of the docks; any firms ships runner would pester or pursue us to help get one of his ships away. Afterwards, when it was all over, they would have their own back if one had been non-cooperative.

Some of the older type of fishermen would never sign on while they had any funds to hand, they disliked leaving behind, anything left unspent, just in case, and their families would have felt cheated if such came to pass.

On one of the first mornings that I visited the dock after this period ashore, I ran into Mr Barnes of the *Cape Matapan*, who was landing, and despite my expectations of a fairly long spell ashore, I was whisked in the office and duly signed on, with no little misgivings. Though the vessel was not a modern one, but was a veteran of many campaigns, this was not the cause of my dislike of her and the skipper was a gentleman who could push the vessel and crew when necessary. The ship was not held to be a lucky one, she never broke any records, or even stepped out from the mob, however she continued to keep going backwards and forwards to distant parts. On my last trip in her we had been the victims of an unprecedented electrical storm, during which the compasses had been ruined and the hull of the vessel had been so magnetized as to baffle the adjusters; she was good at being in the thick of things. She was also a very lazy dreadnought at sea, but one should never deride a ship that carries one safe.

I Sailed in the *Cape Matapan* on Jan. 9th, bound for Iceland. As expected, when we left the Humber, the vessel submerged as if it were a submarine and stayed that way until the engines had ceased their compelling drive to Adlivick. This was one of those trips it would have been better not to have embarked upon. The dreaded black frost, that penetrated into every part of ones body and the ship, that enveloped everything, spread a thick coating of ice on rigging, stays and all it embraced, running up the masts, surmounting the superstructure and even the very clothes we wore. When the cod-line was released, the fish were frozen instantly and to enable the cod-line to be re-tied, hot water had to played on it, keeping it pliable. Every part of the trawl that came out of the water was a block of ice, the scupper doors and holes were blocked with ice and no water could escape. Any water that came on board, even spray, quickly froze solid: fishing soon became impossible and to move through the water was fatal though we could see the faint outline, as the fog drifted in patches like clouds, of the inviting shelter of the fjords.

Every man on board had to fight for their lives with axes, hatch battens, crow bars or anything heavy to hand: even to stand still for a moment or so was fatal. Every time we succeeded in making an impression on the ice, we could crawl a few more yards towards the safety of the fjords: it was that or perish, and the odds were against us. Capsize or float, we had a desperate fight on our hands. Once vessels began to roll over under the sheer weight of ice, the roll gathered momentum and the inevitable was completed in a swift action. Much later, with a change of wind coming from the West, conditions improved and we resumed fishing.

Fortunately, at this time of year, we had little to fear from the great ice barrier or fragments of it: that was safe until the grip of winter relaxed, and allowing icebergs to escape and roam the Arctic. The continual darkness and working always under floodlights was very trying: it was, therefore, reassuring and consoling to see the lights of another vessel and to know that others were suffering in similar conditions.

Touched up with paint, the ship's appearance was enhanced but her conduct was unpredictable, utterly unreliable, she was true yet false, her antics not kittenish, clearly tigerish, she was certainly capricious when about to dive head-long into a menacing sea. She would suddenly change her gait in mid gallop, rear up and await the threatened onslaught or deluge of crashing water. Another wily, very disconcerting deception was to roll heavily, and while we were bracing ourselves for the rebound she would, as if deliberately, dip further, catching everyone off balance.

On one occasion, steaming in a sea of white crested waves, she unexpectedly lurched over on her side. The skipper, on the bridge, stopped me ringing the telegraph to 'slow speed', saying "Don't give in to her, keep going". Slowly, further and further the list developed, until the port side lights were dipping the water and our hearts began thumping, only then did he admit defeat. As the engines almost stopped, she slowly rose again until triumphantly upright. We never quite got accustomed to her tricks and whims. One night on passage, she tossed her 'baby', the ships lifeboat, overboard. A replacement had to be obtained in Iceland. On this trip we landed 900 kit of mixed fish and made £650.

Second trip, bound Iceland. Ran down to Adlivick, twenty odd hours, fishing, chased away at the onset of black frost. Shot off Stalberg Corner and at Snowy Back to Dyra Fjord, 70 baskets, 20 of flats, 40 of ducks. Landed Feb. 21st 750 kit, £750. Left ship.

Sailed in Cape Kanin, March 1st. Bound Iceland. At Iceland passed vessels getting double bags of cod at Akranes and Snowy, towed across Hausa Bay, few flats, S.W. of Stalberg Corner 60 baskets, six of flats, steamed up to Dya Fjord, eight baskets of flats in fifty fath. For two hours tow. Tried Isa Fjord, S.W. of Snowy then N.W. of Akranes. Finished trip N.W. of Vestmann Isles, two hundred baskets, ten of ducks for one hours tow. Landed Wed. Mar. 21st 1,7800 kit, £715. Signed off. Poor markets for catches.

We were scarcely in pocket after all expenses had been paid.

CHAPTER SEVENTEEN

During the shipping depression in the early 30's a new trawler, *Foamflower*, built for a successful skipper to his order placed before this lean time, arrived completed at the dock only to join the fleet of ships laid up awaiting better times. When the depression was lifting a little and more ships were being put back to sea, she was got ready and I signed on, leaving the dock on April 5th, 1932.

When a ship is laid up for a spell in dock, the deterioration of the vessel sets in much faster than if she were at sea, but to a new ship that had never seen the sea, the damage was much worse and more rapid. The masts and rigging with their wire stays had never been stretched in motion and when finally at sea, pitching and rolling, there was trouble all round. The thick wire threaded along the bulwarks to which the fishing gear was chained, parted, and the deck was littered with gear. One after another, the mast stays parted, leaving the masts out of true: all of the wires, ropes and lines had to be renewed. The wooden decks leaked badly until they were soaked through and swelled up tight. The winch had stiffened up through non use and gave trouble during the trip. For a new ship to be in this condition was heartbreaking. Fortunately, the engines, unused to movement, never flagged.

> *At Iceland shot 24 miles N.N.E. of Stalberg Corner, then having poor results, steamed to N. side of the Ness, sixty baskets, several of flats. Dense fog drove us to Thuluk, some haddock, plenty of cod. 1,800 kit on board, left for home. Made £1,080. Markets still poor.*

There is a gap in the diary here and the next entry is as follows:

> Sailed in Cape Barfluer Sept. 12th. 1932. Bound Bear Isle. Nearing the island had reports of continuous N.W. gales, took a chance and a risky gamble in the hopes of finding a lee, steamed on to Spitzberben or Svalbard as it is sometimes called.

Our gamble proved to be a good one: at Betty's Bay, fishing on mud-banks, we found a good lee, close under the icy mountain peaks, in twenty-five to thirty fathoms, and equally important, dense shoals of cod. The cod were exceptionally slimy due to their density, and when gutting them we found their main food was a royal blue seaweed that painted everywhere with its strong colour and smell. We washed the fish several times to get rid of the blue dye and used plenty of ice in stowing. We ate and enjoyed all the fish the cook served up. We tried in fifteen fathom in Magdalen's Bay, with the same result. Within four fishing days we were homeward bound, passing vessels at Bear Isle we had passed going the opposite way, who were still waiting for the gales to moderate. We kept mum. We landed 1,900 kit of nice fat cod but the fish merchants caught the smell of iodine, that was sufficient to discredit our catch, undoubtedly they wanted the plump fish but, as usual, at their price, they would use any excuse for complaint in order to get the price down and it averaged ten shillings a kit.

> Sailed for Bear Island, Oct. 17th. Worked W. and S.E. of Isle. Plenty of cod and wind. Landed 1,640 kit, made £1,078.
>
> Sailed Nov. 9th Bound Bear Island Plenty of fish in the 160 fathom, landed 1,901 kit £490. Shocking, turned to drink.
>
> Left dock Dec. 19th. Christmas Day up to our necks in cod, Bear Island bearing N.W. by N 120 fathom, Landed 1,780 kit, £830.
>
> Sailed Feb. 9th. Headed for Bear Island but bad weather reports, decided to switch to Norwegian coast.

Generally at this time of the year, while the weather could be very bad at the Island, shoals of cod concentrated on the deep slopes of Andenes on the Norwegian coast. There was a good lighthouse to work by, but to set against this was a strong fast flowing tide, and the sea bed fell away steeply from 100 down to 300 fathom in about the width of a main road, and to about a hundred British and foreign vessels that collected there, a main road is exactly what it was. We just had enough ground to shoot the trawl, tow half-an-hour, haul up, and steam back to the starting point and queue in line to shoot again. It was easy to run off the bottom altogether. One year a Hull trawler, the steam trawler Leander was sunk here in collision whilst fishing. There was no letting up the whole of the twenty-four hours, it resembled a race track, but it was much nearer home than most other places. With so many vessels going there and the small area to fish, it was pushing things to try to get two trips from that spot.

One of the most hated places on our voyages to and fro was Spurn Pt. where the tidal race clashed with the sea and fought for supremacy. We called this arrival and departure point, 'liver jar corner'. Prior to special tanks being installed, we sometimes carried up to a hundred barrels for cod livers, to the fishing grounds, allowing for the loss of some on passage, but it was when running home that the real testing time came, turning into the Humber at Spurn, if we succeeded in doing that without losing many, the money was in our pockets, it was most annoying to have carried them thousands of miles, only to lose any rounding this last obstacle on the final home stretch.

On our next trip, nearing the S.E. coast of Iceland, we picked up a cryptic, tense message, flashed by radio from one Grimsby trawler to another. "Finding it poor at Seydis Fjord, come."

There had been no time to swing the direction finder on the sender, but headed straight for that area, no one stays on no fish, and none broadcasts when on it. Plainly he wanted no one but his pal. Our hunch to go there and our luck in intercepting the radio call proved very fortunate indeed. We were soon towing towards the lights of a vessel about four miles off the land and were knee deep in plaice with a sprinkling of haddock, long enough to get an exceptionally nice catch on board and on landing and make a record in earnings, over £4,000.

About this time it was decided to make a trip to the Newfoundland Banks, carrying sufficient fuel was the biggest problem. We rounded the tip of Scotland and departed Cape Wrath for nine solid days thumping into a head wind across the Atlantic. On arriving on the banks, the weather was foul and we headed for some smoother water in the vicinity of the Gulf of St. Lawrence. Fishing was fairly good, but the biggish size of everything was surprising, even dabs. Later we got on the banks and took enough cod on board to head for home and face another long tedious slog. Expenses were high and those grounds were abandoned until several years later when the larger freezer trawlers came along.

In one ship, on passage to Bear Island in stormy weather, the first night out, my watch relieved the mate's, he told me that he had been on the point of calling the skipper to the bridge. I was very apprehensive the way the vessel was reacting to the following seas that lifted our stern, roared and raced past in a white mass of foam, sweeping along both sides and into the blackness ahead. We must have been doing well over twelve knots. I said it was crazy, that the skipper could take the watch, not me, and immediately called him from his berth. Peering round the bridge through sleepy eyes, he grumbled, "What's the matter, getting the wind up". He looked round again, then using the voice pipe, instructed the engineer down below to ease in half-a-dozen revolutions. As he descended the steps to his quarters the expected happened. It was only the crest of a wave that thundered on board, but it clean swept the decks, forced the wheelhouse door open and deluged his quarters as he fell in a heap.

Unfortunately, it was not only his place that shipped water, there was the after cabin, galley and engine room before the water rushed forward under the whaleback and flooded the forecastle. The skipper was soon confronted by an angry watch below, resentful of being baptised in their bunks. Needless to remark, that skipper did not carry me again; our dislike was mutual. I was no mutineer, but that night I'd have cheerfully swung for him. The accusation he had thrown at me was unforgivable; no true seaman would level that against another who had the lives of his crew and their wives and children in his hands. To me he was the lowest of the low, beneath contempt. I was always aware of my responsibilities in this direction, would that some skippers had not let their greed overcome their humane instincts. It was a man's world and not all could live up to it.

With some it was simply the consolation of a bottle, understandable when one has been reared since birth on this phenomenon of the human race. In times of great stress and utter isolation it could bring temporary relief, but reality still had to be faced eventually, no matter how long one dodged the issue. In Arctic going vessels the Customs allowed a little over a bottle of spirits on board per man, for medicinal purposes really, it was a very fortunate crew that saw half a bottle in most ships. To be under the influence of alcohol at sea could easily lead to the loss of ones life or that of others, and a sober skipper was essential.

It was a body and soul satisfying challenging way of life, a sharing with others, experiencing the wonders of nature and enduring terrific hardships together in that same comradeship that so many came to know and marvel about during the two world wars.

The whole of a fisherman's way of life at sea needed drastically changing to make it more humane in many ways, yet these ways had gone on for over a century in the customary methods, a life taken up from long family connections with the sea. Gradually, inevitably, over the years the vessels improved in sea worthiness, size, living space, from sail to engines, oil and gas lighting to electric, many improvements came about. Though the Board of Trade had always laid down the rules and regulations for the vessels, there had never been any organization of the crews, nor had there ever been any serious dispute in the industry, therefore it was amazing that one act of the trawlers brought the first trouble and concerted action of the crews in that they left their vessels in port and refused to sail until the matter was settled. The cause of the dispute was the interference by the owners in the collection and disposal of the fish livers and the oil money realized from them.

Over many years the livers taken from the fish were saved and stored in forty gallon wooden casks, stowed on the deck and called liver jars. These were the crew's perks, their own to dispose of, and had always been a long standing right of theirs. It was no mean task to carry a good number of these casks lashed to the bulwarks on the open deck and carry them safely throughout the voyage. Many fishermen were injured in attempting to re-stow those that were washed adrift in foul weather. In the large trawlers more than a hundred jars would be carried on deck. Spurn Point at the mouth of the Humber was known as 'liver jar corner' so many were lost there as vessels rounded the point in bad weather to enter the last stretch for home. But the days of the liver jars came to an end.

By 1950 most trawlers had been equipped with boilers on board to render the livers down to oil at sea and run into tanks installed below decks, quite an improvement on the previous method, before this, the oil had been produced in a factory onshore. Naturally, the owners took over the collection and distribution of the processed oil, and understandably the crews rose up to fight against this take over of what had always been considered their rights. The whole fishing industry was brought to a standstill for weeks until an agreement was reached. The Transport and General Workers' Union intervened in the dispute and put some re-organization of the crew into effect. In such a large industry there was a great need for sound administration and various sections joined or formed groups, which brought some improvements in conditions of service at sea. From 1950 also the Ministry of Fisheries took a much more concerned supervision of the industry, as indeed they had to over the next decade or so when disputes with other countries arose until the whole world became alive to and involved in fish conservation and fishing rights.

None-the-less, no power on earth could harness or regulate against the tremendous and overwhelming forces of the Arctic and it continued to take its toll of life and ships of those venturing into its waters.

At the beginning of 1968, three of the most modern and powerful trawlers from the port of Hull and their crews, save one man from one vessel, were "lost at sea". Reports of the weather they encountered at the time were as follows:

"Lashed by gales".

"The worst weather for many years".

"Vessels in the area sheltering from a force 12 hurricane were struggling for survival".

"The victims died in a white hell".

"Exceptional combination of hurricane winds, corresponding sea conditions and heavy icing".

A scourge of the Arctic, much to be feared, was the dreaded frostbite, which struck chiefly at any exposed part of the body. The affected part would turn white and become dead. Frantic rubbing with snow could restore the circulation, but, if it failed, the affected part remained dead and withered away, similar to leprosy, it struck unnoticed, until its deadly work had begun.

Whilst it was never intended to list the numerous tragedies over the years that led to the loss of vessels and crews, we should not forget the loss of the modern trawlers off the North Cape, Iceland in January 1953, namely *Roderigo* and *Lorella* in heavy icing conditions, with all hands, and the most recent loss early in 1974 of the super trawler *Gaul*, which disappeared with all hands off Norway. The Arctic seems to be at its most vicious at the turn of the year. Little wonder Kingston-upon-Hull was well equipped with orphanages.

After 1950 the processing and deep freezing of catches became big business. Huge surplus supplies could be dealt with to cover the lean periods. The advantages far outweighed the disadvantages over the years, so it is proving in the fish farming methods being carried on today and will continue to do so in the fishing industry of the future.

APPENDIX 1

In 1924 at the age of 14, Ernest started at sea, bound for Iceland. These were some of the vessels on which he sailed after sitting and passing his Boatswain's ticket on 13th August 1930.

Vessel		Crew	Sailing Dates
Steam Trawler	Cape Melville		1930
	Thomas Hardy	Skipper - Harry Archer	1930
	Chalcedony	Skipper - Ralph Cobby	1930
	Unknown (new)	Owner/Skipper - Iceland John	
		Mate - (Viking) Martin Dalgreevs	
		Boatswain - Russian Alex	
	Cassio	Skipper - Frank Furnley	10/06/31
	Cape Finisterre	Skipper - Jimmy Myres	1931
	Cape Matapan	Skipper - Jack Barns	09/01/32
	Cape Kanin	Skipper - Albert Harmer	01/03/32
	Foam Flower		05/04/32
	Cape Barfleur		12/09/32

Service with Hudson Bros

Vessel		Position held	Sailing dates
Steam Trawler	Cape Barfleur	Boatswain	14/06/37 - 13/08/37
	Cape Grisnez	"	14/08/37 - 06/10/37
	Cape Barfleur	"	07/10/37 - 01/01/38
	Cape Barfleur	"	03/01/38 - 30/03/38
	Cape Barfleur	"	07/04/38 - 11/07/38
	Cape Barfleur	"	16/09/38 - 06/10/38
	Cape Argona	"	13/10/38 - 03/01/39
	Cape Argona	"	17/04/39 - 29/06/39
	Cape Argona	"	01/07/39 - 21/07/39
	Cape Barracouta	"	02/08/39 - 22/08/39

Vessel		Position held	Sailing dates
R/N Service	Europa	Seaman	09/09/40 - 10/09/40
	(Edwina) Badger	Leading Seaman	11/09/40 - 04/06/41
	Europa	"	05/06/41 - 02/10/41
	(Irantella) Caroline	"	03/10/41 - 19/01/42
	Europa	P.S.G.L.	20/01/42 - 25/02/42
	Europa	Petty Officer (ps)	26/02/42 - 21/03/42
	(Soisra) Euphrates	"	22/03/42 - 30/04/43
	Jana	"	01/05/43 - 21/01/45
	Europa	"	22/01/45 - 16/04/45
	(Ferella) Porcupine	"	17/04/45 - 23/06/45
	Bacchante		24/06/45 - 04/08/45
	Europa		05/08/45 - 12/11/45

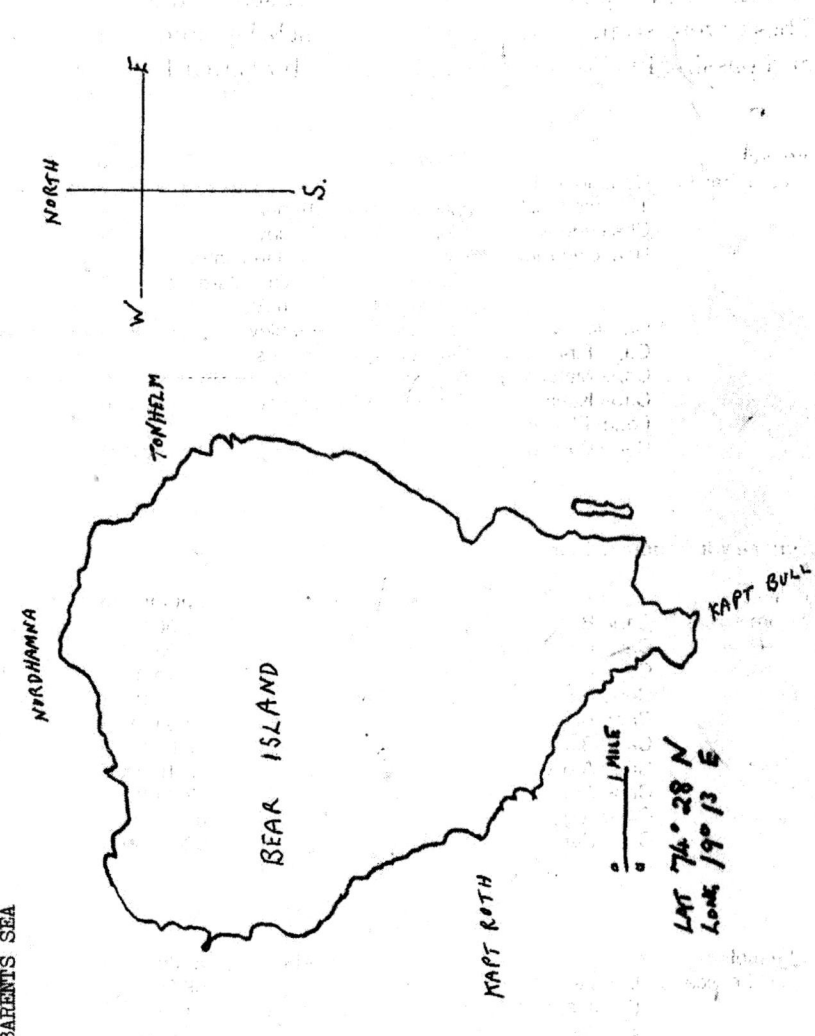

Ernest Cleveland